GUND Partnership

GUND Partnership

Introduction by Paul Goldberger

Published in Australia in 2008 by
The Images Publishing Group Pty Ltd
ABN 89 059 734 431
6 Bastow Place, Mulgrave, Victoria 3170, Australia
Tel: +61 3 9561 5544 Fax: +61 3 9561 4860
books@imagespublishing.com
www.imagespublishing.com

Copyright © The Images Publishing Group Pty Ltd 2008
The Images Publishing Group Reference Number: 757

National Library of Australia Cataloguing-in-Publication entry:

Gund Partnership 1994–2007.

Includes index.
ISBN 978 186470 273 6 (hbk.).

1. Gund Partnership. 2. Architectural firms – United
States. 3. Architecture, Modern. I. Mahar, Christa. II.
Title. (Series: Master architect series).

725.0973

Edited by Christa Mahar

Designed by Carlos Ridruejo

Digital production by Splitting Image Colour Studio Pty Ltd, Australia

Printed by Everbest Printing Co. Ltd., in Hong Kong/China

IMAGES has included on its website a page for special notices in relation to this
and our other publications. Please visit www.imagespublishing.com.

Contents

6   Graham Gund: The Architecture of Civitas and Joy
by Paul Goldberger

Selected Projects 1994–2007

16   Middle School Complex Hathaway Brown School Shaker Heights, Ohio
24   Carol and John Butler Aquatic Center Hathaway Brown School Shaker Heights, Ohio
30   Horace Mann School Riverdale, New York
38   The Ensworth School Nashville, Tennessee
48   Library, Mathematics and Science Building The Taft School Watertown, Connecticut
54   The Fannie Cox Center for Science, Math and Technology Friends' Central School Wynnewood, Pennsylvania
58   Visual Arts Building and Library Lawrenceville School Lawrenceville, New Jersey
64   Young Israel Synagogue Brookline, Massachusetts
70   Center for Dramatic Arts University of North Carolina Chapel Hill, North Carolina
78   Inn at Celebration Celebration, Florida
82   WaterSound Bridges WaterSound, Florida
86   Eaton Center Kenyon College Gambier, Ohio
90   Dimond Library University of New Hampshire Durham, New Hampshire
96   Mathematics and Science Complex Kenyon College Gambier, Ohio
104   Jeppesen Science Center Berwick Academy South Berwick, Maine
108   Jackson Library Berwick Academy South Berwick, Maine
112   Music Building Kenyon College Gambier, Ohio
118   North Shore Center for the Performing Arts Skokie, Illinois
122   Campbell Center for the Performing Arts The Groton School Groton, Massachusetts
126   Carol and Park B. Smith Hall College of the Holy Cross Worcester, Massachusetts
134   Burton D. Morgan Hall Denison University Granville, Ohio
142   Talbot Hall of Biological Science Denison University Granville, Ohio
148   Baker Science Center Episcopal High School Alexandria, Virginia
152   Summer Residence Nantucket, Massachusetts
158   Five Lowell Street Residence Cambridge, Massachusetts
166   Celebration Office Building Celebration, Florida
172   Celebration High School Celebration, Florida
180   Cleveland Botanical Garden Cleveland, Ohio
192   Law School Library Addition Case Western Reserve University Cleveland, Ohio
196   EuroDisney's International Retail and Manufacturers' Showcase Paris, France
202   The Waverly at Lake Eola Orlando, Florida
206   National Association of Realtors Washington, D.C.
216   Thompson Library Addition and Renovation The Ohio State University Columbus, Ohio
222   Lois Foster Wing at the Rose Art Museum Waltham, Massachusetts
230   Kenyon Athletic Center Kenyon College Gambier, Ohio
250   Copley Square Subway Station Boston, Massachusetts
252   Housing Study Tufts University Medford, Massachusetts
254   Chemistry Building Study Denison University Granville, Ohio
256   Visual Arts Center University of Massachusetts Amherst, Massachusetts
258   Newton North High School Newton, Massachusetts

262   Collaboration by Design *by Hilary Lewis*
264   Firm Profile
272   Bibliography
278   Awards
280   Project Chronology
286   Acknowledgements
288   Index

Graham Gund: The Architecture of Civitas and Joy

Paul Goldberger

Few notions in contemporary architecture are as misused, misunderstood and misapplied as the idea of contextualism, the belief that a building should respond to its surroundings, or context. And few architects offer as much hope for an enlightened and consistently imaginative approach to contextualism as Graham Gund. Gund has never accepted the easy view that contextualism means replication, and his architecture studiously avoids the glibness of imitation. A Gund building never looks like the building next door, even if it is an addition to that building. Yet nothing guides Gund's design sensibility more than the nature of the buildings that are already there. He sees his mission as reading those buildings, picking up subtle cues from them, and then designing new in a way that neither imitates nor defies, but enriches through a kind of harmonic counterpoint.

The starting point for Graham Gund is always what is there. That is always his touchstone, far more than any theoretical precept or stylistic preference—indeed, one might almost say that in Gund's way of making architecture, the notion of what is there becomes, for all intents and purposes, a theoretical precept in itself. It is a philosophical statement: the real is what matters. Architecture is a quest to make this world better, not to establish another one. Yet if starting with what is there defines Gund's sensibility, it does not limit his imagination, because he expresses the concept of what is there in such broad and generous terms. If his buildings are anti-utopian, realistic solutions rather than idealized forms, they are no less celebrations of inventiveness. Even more than it is practical, Gund's work is joyful.

Graham Gund's designs are also invariably assertions of the view that a work of architecture is an element in a larger entity, part both of the literal community of buildings that are its physical neighbors, and of the conceptual community of buildings that are its architectural peers. Gund's buildings are expressions of civitas. He designs as if to say that for architecture, as for people, there are obligations of citizenship, and they

are fulfilled best not by disappearing into quiet anonymity, but by staking a strong, identifiable presence that takes as its core value respect for fellow citizens.

For Gund, then, context is far more than just a matter of architectural style. It is sometimes not even a matter of buildings, and is probably much better thought of as a larger quest to establish sense of place. He sometimes seems as interested in urban design as he is in architecture, and every one of Gund's designs makes some sort of statement about urbanity. It may be a matter of making fresh and engaging connections to the surrounding streets, or of conceiving of a building as a kind of punctuation mark within the urban fabric; or it may be a matter of envisioning the building's circulation as streets in themselves, and its major spaces urban piazzas: the building as metaphor for urban life. The one thing Gund seems constitutionally unable to do is to design a building as a pure, abstract object, floating in imaginary space, disconnected from either physical or social context. The idea of place, for Gund, is so powerfully real that it always sets the tone. His great skill as an architect is to interpret that tone in consistently resourceful ways.

It is no accident that a tremendous amount of Gund's work has been on school and university campuses. He seems naturally to understand that the campus is itself a model for the city, and that the challenge of designing academic buildings today lies as much in preserving and enhancing campus fabric is it does in fulfilling the practical demands of a building program. He appears also to know that school buildings often have the paradoxical need both to look backward, toward older works of architecture that exert a powerful hold on an institution's sense of itself, and forward, since no institution, however respectful of tradition it may be, is inclined to send a signal that it is not prepared for a changing new world. Gund's best work is characterized by a sense of balance between these countervailing forces: looking back and looking ahead; connecting both literally and symbolically to the existing context; and offering a symbol of the new. It is not easy to do all of these things at the same time, while also fulfilling the demands of a complex program, and it is more difficult still to orchestrate all of these conflicting pressures into a coherent work of architecture that has strength and clarity, and does not feel like the product of compromise.

No project makes the point more clearly than Gund's new Middle School for Hathaway Brown School in Shaker Heights, Ohio. It is an exceptionally complex project, since the school, based in a handsome and mature suburban community, consisted of a number of older, connected buildings that had grown in a confusing and uneven pattern, and with their long corridors had begun to take on the rambling nature of an old airport concourse. Gund needed to expand the school substantially and give the complex coherence and order without significantly altering the older wings—to change the school while keeping it the same, in other words.

His solution, which consists of a four-story high, L-shaped addition built around a new, glass-enclosed central hall, manages to turn what had been the bête noir of the original building, circulation, into the central idea of the new one.

The new hall, which rises to the building's full height and culminates in a vaulted gambrel roof of glass, is paneled in maple, and is full of natural light. It is an exhilarating space, and it is not surprising that it quickly became the school's town square, gathering place and symbol. The classrooms all open off the hall, and open stairs rise through it, assuring that every student passes through the space several times a day. Like all good public spaces, it serves both as casual meeting place and as an emblem of the larger place of which it is a part.

Gund in effect changed the center of gravity at Hathaway Brown, shifting it so the campus as a whole was oriented more toward the new hall. But he was cognizant of not displacing the old, and also managed to re-orient the entry sequence to the whole campus, creating a new approach drive that enhances the dignity of the older buildings more than it shows off his own. And he also added an aquatic center in a separate wing with an exceptionally handsome exterior that skillfully mediates between the differing scales of the school and the suburban houses on an adjacent street.

The architecture of the new wings at Hathaway Brown is, like much of Gund's work, precisely poised between traditional and modern. The buildings are constructed of brick, limestone and glass; there are dormers and bay windows, as in the older buildings, and the scale is consistent with the older portions of the school. Every surface has a rich texture. But there is no doubt, even at a casual glance, that these buildings are new. There is more glass, the details are crisper, and there is a sense of energy that is nowhere present in the older wings. But it is energy in repose, as if Gund were doing all he could to make for a serene juxtaposition.

The underlying themes of the additions to Hathaway Brown—the establishment of a relationship to older buildings through materials, scale and texture, as well as the organization of a building complex into a coherent and readable pattern—are repeated in several of Gund's other educational projects, like the Horace Mann School in Riverdale, New York; the music building and the grouping of science buildings at Kenyon College in Gambier, Ohio; the Visual Arts Building at Lawrenceville School in Lawrenceville, New Jersey; and Smith Hall, at the College of the Holy Cross in Worcester, Massachusetts, to name only a few. In each case Gund was committed to restoring and renewing campus fabric, and in each case he produced a building that subtly extended certain architectural themes of older buildings while clearly establishing itself as new. Holy Cross is particularly notable, with a red brick exterior that more closely resembles nineteenth-century industrial structures than most of Gund's work does, and manages to look both appropriate for its setting and exceptionally inviting. The library-chapel within is one of Gund's best interior spaces, at once crisp and tranquil, with tall glass windows that loosely echo the stained glass of Frank Lloyd Wright.

At Kenyon, a different set of conditions applied. Gund attended this college as an undergraduate, had known its unusually beautiful campus, bisected by a long gravel path flanked by rows of trees, for decades, and had been troubled by the extent to which its fabric had been disturbed by insensitive intrusions. His science quadrangle consists of two new buildings and one renovated one, all sheathed in sandstone, with large vertical windows to loosely echo the Gothic architecture of many of the older buildings of the campus, including a much admired building that forms the fourth side of the quadrangle. What is equally important, however, is what is not there: Gund's plan called for the removal of a mediocre building from the 1960s that blocked the connection between his quadrangle and the central portion of the campus. It was a case of demolition rather than construction being used to knit the fabric together.

For the music building, which is technically an addition to a Neoclassical building that housed little more than an auditorium behind a columned facade, Gund allowed the old structure to maintain pride of place while enhancing it with a new building that serves as both backdrop and counterpoint to it. This is one of his most subtle urban interventions, and one of his most successful. The addition repeats none of the classical details of the old building save for the presence of a single column, more tapered than the original, that marks the corner entrance of the new wing, a sign, like so many of Gund's best gestures, of both old and new at the same time. Within is a small recital hall, paneled in maple and awash with natural light, that is one of the finest small spaces Gund has designed anywhere.

For a new theater arts building at the University of North Carolina at Chapel Hill, as at Kenyon, Gund's starting point was also an older building that needed to be significantly expanded,

but this time it was a poorly organized modern academic building, set on a diagonal, its architecture more like that of the 1960s building at Kenyon that Gund demolished than the classical one he celebrated. Removing the building was not an option in North Carolina, and Gund expanded it with a curving facade of glass that covered its awkward geometries and served as a transition to the grid of the campus. Gund wrapped the facade in a modernist colonnade, topped with a clerestory.

But what of campuses in which there is neither a cherished context to be renewed, as at Kenyon, or a piece of bad architecture to be neutralized, as at Chapel Hill? Gund was asked by the Ensworth School, a long-established independent school in Nashville, to design an entirely new high school campus on a 124-acre site, formerly occupied by a farm, that has a mountainous, undeveloped edge on one side and suburban neighborhoods on the other. His solution, which he convinced a conservative board that had originally sought a by-the-book, Georgian-style design, to accept, was to design a set of modern buildings organized in the pattern of a traditional campus. The architecture is what might be called Gundian modern, which is to say that while it lacks any of the specific details of a historical style, it is richly textured and carefully scaled. There is plenty of glass, but there are never sleek, flat curtain walls of glass. The campus has a central clock tower that could almost be a piece of 1930s, stripped-down classicism, rendered in red brick, and an arts building whose facade is a series of three identical gables. The quadrangle is asymmetrical, and it rambles in the way that much larger campuses might be expected to do, substituting,

in effect, complexity of space and richness of texture for the resonance of time.

Over the years, Gund's version of modernism has become, gradually but steadily, more overtly modernist. So far as historicist architects are concerned he was always a modernist, of course, since he never engaged in the direct replication of historical style that they do, but his version of contextual architecture has sometimes seemed so respectful of older buildings that it is not surprising that, at least to modernist architects, Gund could often be viewed as a more traditional architect than he was. It has been more difficult to make that mistake in the last few years, as the modernist elements in Gund's buildings have become more assertive, and as he has broadened his notions of contextualism still more.

Gund has explained the more explicitly modernist aspect of his work as coming in large part from a desire to make buildings lighter, which in his case means both giving them more natural light and making them feel less massive and weighty. Glass seems to Gund now as red brick was a few years ago, which is to say it is the material he seems most comfortable using as his primary form of expression. It has been the principal material—indeed, the defining material—of three recent buildings that are among the finest in his career: the Kenyon Athletic Center, the Cleveland Botanical Garden, and the National Association of Realtors headquarters in Washington, D.C.

The Kenyon Athletic Center, completed in 2006, marks a significant departure both for the architect and his client. The earlier projects Gund had done for Kenyon, the music building, the science quadrangle and a small white clapboard administrative building, were all to one degree or another examples of Gund's highly textured, strongly contextual modernism. The athletic center, an enormous structure that embraces an indoor running track, multiple gymnasia, several pools, tennis courts and a fitness center under a vast, vaulted roof, is at the edge of campus, not adjacent or even visible from any of Kenyon's older structures. Gund wrapped the building almost entirely in glass. The roof soars over the building's various elements, supported by a series of huge, white-painted trusses. The athletic center's wide-ranging program makes it, internally, almost a city in itself, yet its glass walls and ample supply of natural light make it feel connected completely to the outdoors. The building is at once monumental and light, muscular and lyrical.

The botanical garden in Cleveland, unlike the Kenyon athletic center, is an addition to an existing structure. But the charge was to transform the institution from a relatively modest garden center to a full-fledged conservatory and biome, a program that required Gund to build at a scale that would render the original building clearly subservient to his own. He produced an entry pavilion that, as with many of his educational buildings, ordered a complex sequence of spaces into a clear and logical processional movement, and then added an 18,000-square-foot conservatory, its irregular geometries loosely based on the shape of a quartz crystal. The space is abstract, but powerful and clear, and as benignly monumental, in its way, as the athletic center at Kenyon. Architects have been tinkering with the form of the glass conservatory for a century-and-a-half, and Gund's mountain-like glass form in Cleveland ranks as one of the more notable re-interpretations of the conservatory in our time.

In Washington, Gund had neither a campus nor an older building to contend with, but he had the unusual city plan of L'Enfant's Washington, whose diagonal streets yielded in this instance an exceptionally difficult site a few blocks from the Capitol. Essentially a narrow triangular island, it had previously been occupied by a gas station, and numerous developers had rejected it as too awkward to yield a workable building. Gund's appetite for problematic contexts led him to embrace the challenge of building a small office tower on this small site, and he produced what is surely his finest commercial building anywhere, a tower of bluish, aquamarine glass with facades that curve subtly toward a prow-like point. The building's form narrows from a 60 foot width at one end to roughly 10 feet at the prow. Rising at the prow to anchor and punctuate the entire composition is a mast of exposed steel truss work that seems like late Frank Lloyd Wright married to high-tech.

The National Association of Realtors is a building of glass in a city of masonry, a colorful building in a city of bland, neutral structures, a building of curves in a city built mostly in straight lines, and an avowedly modernist object in a city that has come increasingly to use historical references as an architectural crutch. Not the least of its accomplishments is that it is also the first building in Washington constructed to LEED standards of responsible environmental design.

The National Association of Realtors building seems, at first glance, to be more object-like than most of Gund's work, but it could not be more appropriate for its site, and indeed, its form could not have been generated by anything other than its site. In this sense it has something in common with a pair of buildings that, outwardly, could not be more different from it, the rambling houses Gund has designed in Cambridge and Nantucket. These two, like the building in Washington, are eccentric as forms, and for all the wood siding in the Cambridge house and shingles in the one in Nantucket, neither of them seems at first glance to be intimately connected to its surroundings. Yet in each case, the unusual shapes are responses to sites that, in their own ways, have as many constraints as the site in Washington. The Cambridge house is on an unusual, large lot tucked into a mid-block behind other houses, and it manages to be both expansive and tightly enclosed, both outward and inward looking, as the site demands. The Nantucket house overlooks the ocean, but its site is surrounded by conservation land, and the challenge was to fulfill the demands of a large and complex program without creating a structure that would overwhelm this delicate landscape. Both houses are disciplined and whimsical, dignified and celebratory, all at the same time, which for any work of architecture is no small accomplishment. Like so much of Gund's work, they emanate contentment but not complacency, and they each manage to honor not only the life that goes on within them, but the larger place of which they are a part. ▪

Paul Goldberger is the Architecture Critic for *The New Yorker* and holds the Joseph Urban Chair of Design and Architecture at The New School in New York. He is the author of numerous books on architecture, including *Up From Zero: Politics, Architecture, and the Rebuilding of New York.* In 1984, while writing for *The New York Times,* he was awarded the Pulitzer Prize for Distinguished Criticism, the highest award in journalism.

Selected Projects 1994–2007

Originally chartered in 1876, Hathaway Brown is Ohio's oldest college preparatory school for girls. When the campus was built, the graceful older buildings were planned with generous windows, filling the interior corridors and rooms with precious natural light. Although the buildings were beautifully crafted, they lacked public spaces for gathering and were characterized by an extensive amount of corridor space.

As the Middle and Upper Schools each expanded, their coexistence in an historic Walker and Weeks building began to compromise programmatic offerings. The solution features a distinct new home for the Middle School, organized by a covered indoor courtyard. By creating an L-shaped 61,000-square-foot addition to the original building with a central enclosed Great Hall, the primary circulation becomes an engaging experience of community. The Great Hall connects the historic buildings of the campus with a new heart of circulation across multiple levels.

Locating the "L" of the new wings in the northwest corner of the campus and establishing a new entry axis from the north reorients the entire campus circulation. A new entry drive focuses on the main facade of the original building. The entry sequence has been streamlined, with parking distributed to the sides of the building and a new drop-off circle to organize the entries of the Upper School, Middle School and gymnasium.

The main tenants in the new wing are the fifth through eighth grades, conceived as "neighborhoods" on levels two and three. The neighborhood is

Middle School Complex Hathaway Brown School, Shaker Heights, Ohio
1998–2001

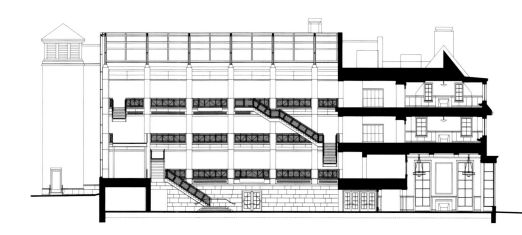

1

2

3

N

a central building block of the Middle School experience and conceived as an extension of the classroom environment, with ample breakout space, lockers, and tables for collaborative group work. Two distinct neighborhood areas are located on each of the middle levels, supported by a common room for special curricular projects. Middle School classrooms feature both carpeted areas and tiled flooring with moveable desks and soft furniture to accommodate hands-on learning projects of this age group. The splitting of the Middle School on two levels and the pairing of grades on each floor creates an intentional home base and identity for each grade.

This reimagining of the Middle School identity allowed for expansion of the Upper School in place, as well as the location of three fully equipped science laboratories in the new construction. School-wide student activities spaces are also a key

Previous page A ceramic fritted glass canopy covers the Great Hall, washing the interiors with filtered light and celebrating activities throughout the day and evening.

1 A reorganized campus circulation, including the separation of younger and older students and a new front door drop-off, helped to ease pressure on the surrounding fine-grain residential neighborhood.
2 The Middle School addition features a rhythm of dormers and bays that complement the architectural vocabulary of the existing school.
3 Ground floor plan: **a** Great Hall; **b** dining hall; **c** servery; **d** scene shop; **e** music room; **f** black box theater

Next page 1 Natural light is a backdrop to learning in both the classrooms and informal gathering spaces within the neighborhoods.
2 Section through the courtyard shows the relationship between spaces.

1

element of the program, including a renovated arts complex and a 300-seat dining facility (sized to accommodate the entire Lower, Middle or Upper School students at one sitting) on the lower level of the addition. The atrium is the school's public square, and a place where the entire school can meet outside of the classroom.

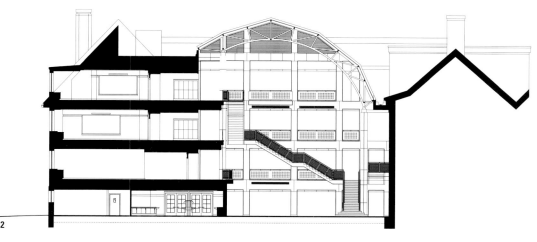

2

1 The flexible layout and moveable furnishings in the Middle School allow for the widest range of uses and activities.
2 The Upper School science classrooms feature a transparent fume hood for demonstration purposes and flexibility in teaching styles.

Next page While the Great Hall organizes the entire school-wide campus circulation, it also connects at the third level, allowing visitors to sequence throughout the entire campus without changing elevation.

The Great Hall connects all four floors of the Middle School addition and serves as the hub of daily school life, a spectacular setting for special events and school-wide gatherings, and a covered "outdoor" space.

The massing, materials and details of the new construction are carefully modulated to complement the Neo-Gothic/Arts and Crafts style of the existing campus architecture, while simultaneously capturing a distinctly contemporary flavor that reflects the intellectual dynamism of the community. ■

1 Each floor is organized by a series of distinct neighborhoods, which include generous meeting and study spaces.
2 The dining hall features two-story windows that offer a glimpse into the bustling life of the school.

1

Learning environments are pushing beyond the classroom to enrich all aspects of the student's life and their development as young adults. At the Hathaway Brown School in Shaker Heights, Ohio, the mission is to foster and promote the mind, body and spirit of the young women who attend.

The new aquatic center provides learning opportunities and challenges for all ages, from the first-time swimmer to college-level competition. The location is at the southern terminus of the campus, adjoining the existing athletic facilities. The siting takes advantage of natural light and proximity to playing fields and green space, and creates clear views across the landscape.

The simple form of this light and airy structure is premised as a large garden pavilion surrounded by nature. Its location and material expression contribute to the sense of being virtually outdoors.

When this campus was first built, the English Gothic buildings were planned with generous large windows with divided panes of glass, filling the interior corridors and rooms with streams of light. The pool pavilion similarly uses large areas of glass, divided by brick piers. Simple materials and their clarity of expression become an elegant backdrop for learning, similar in fashion to the school's original Walker and Weeks building.

Carol and John Butler Aquatic Center Hathaway Brown School, Shaker Heights, Ohio
2001–2005

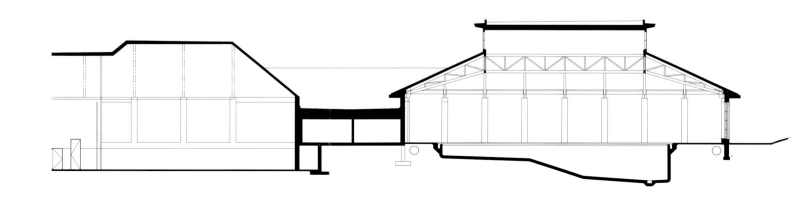

Previous page Mechanical
system supply and diffusers are
incorporated around the pool and
in the bench seating below the
windows. Exposed trusswork,
painted metal decking, electrical
lighting, sprinklers and audio
systems are highly coordinated to
become the finish ceiling surfaces.

Next page Stone and brick
piers provide a contemporary
interpretation of historic masonry
detailing found on the existing
campus buildings.

Overleaf Set gently into a rolling
landscape setting, the new pavilion
echoes a varied pattern of adjacent
buildings.

In the graceful structure
of the roof, a monitor with
a diffused glass clerestory
floods the center of the
pool with controlled natural light. The perimeter
glazing utilizes a graduated
ceramic fritted pattern that
allows less light in at the
top of the wall and blocks
the harsh glare of the
direct sun. More light is
allowed to penetrate lower
in the window, permitting
views out. On a cloudy
day, this treatment makes
the outside light appear
much brighter. The glaz-
ing beckons visitors in, but
also protects against glare
for the activities within the
pool interior.

The vertical proportions
are in keeping with the
larger surrounding context
of athletic buildings. The
blending of traditional
and modern expression
mediates the diversity of
architectural styles on the
campus. ■

Horace Mann School Riverdale, New York
2000–2002

Strong enrollment growth and expanded curricular opportunities had put pressure on the historic school buildings of this private independent school in Riverdale, New York. From a Master Plan in the early 1990s, the school undertook several projects to strengthen and separate its middle division. With the completion of the Middle School construction, the Upper Division was housed in an historic building along West 246th Street and a 1960s-era theater structure at the corner of Tibbett Avenue. The facilities were severely deficient and provided only a fraction of the space needed for the high school.

The project encompasses upgrade and modernization of the Collegiate Gothic historic buildings, together with construction of two distinct new buildings. The building program includes a new theater, administration and library building, as well as a significant new front entry to the entire 100-year-old campus.

The concept was to establish a revitalized presence for the school at the intersection of two major thoroughfares by creating a strong new front entry expression and knitting together the historic architecture of its main classroom building, Tillinghast Hall, with new construction. With its solid front of hewn gray granite and its elegantly arched leaded windows, the original Tillinghast Hall (1914) was the symbolic face of the school, echoing its mission, tradition and purpose. The crowded classrooms and hallways of the interior, however, accommodated in excess of 700 students, more than twice the population for which it was designed. In addition, the pedagogical approach and philosophy of the school had dramatically changed in the intervening years, making the physical space functionally obsolete.

Previous page The scale of the existing streetwall is maintained along West 246th Street to mediate between the historic buildings of the school and new construction.

1 Prior to the expansion, the school lacked an identifiable front door and cohesive character. The new entry is composed of twin towers flanking a two-story library and generous lobby.
2 Site plan shows the new corner intervention, remaking the campus hierarchy and entry sequence.

1

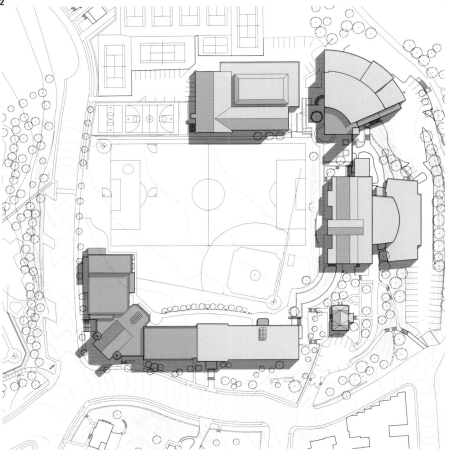

2

The design solution respects the original campus planning principles of the complex by re-establising hierarchy of buildings and clarifying internal organization. While Tillinghast Hall maintains its physical exterior identity on the campus, the venerable old building was completely reimagined. The penthouse of the three-story building was removed and the interior was completely gutted. The replanned interior features wider hallways and windows, which transfer more

natural light into larger classrooms. Still intact are two original staircases and a restored Elizabethan-style classroom with dark oak paneling.

A major component of the integrated revitalization plan is the demoli-tion and replacement of a 1960s-era building, Gross Hall, with a new three-story building. The main entrance contains a new library, 650-seat theater, and dramatic entrance lobby. The library is char-acterized by an elegantly lit and spacious reading

1 An historic classroom with the Harkness table was restored.
2 A new classroom in Tillinghast Hall utilizes the same pedagogical approach.
3 Entry level plan **a** theater wing; **b** administration and lobby; **c** classroom wing

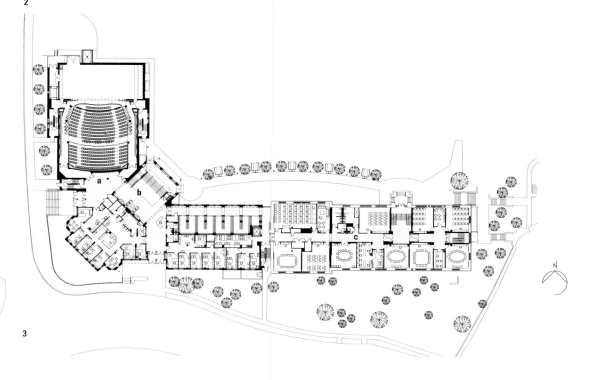

1

2

1 The corner lobby is an open living room and social center for the school and knits together the historic building with the new. **2** Shelving for books in the two-story library reading room is located flush to the dividing wall, maximizing a feeling of openness within the circulation.

Next page The 650-seat theater is equipped with a sophisticated sound system, computer controlled lighting booth and full fly loft.

Overleaf The grand entry stair of the lobby looks out onto the athletic fields, reinforcing the dynamic between enclosure and expansion.

room, which blends the historic with the new. Twin towers flank the library for a two-story grand reading room with windows that bring in light from above.

The lobby is the organizing main entry to the school and also acts as a forecourt to the protected athletic fields within. The facade composition creates a coherent new streetwall along two major thoroughfares and features a complementary richness of materials to the historic buildings of the school. ■

THE OLSHAN LOBBY

This independent day school planned to develop an entirely separate new upper school campus for grades 9–12. The challenge of siting the extensive program for the new high school campus, together with its related athletic fields, parking and circulation roads, was exacerbated by its historically significant site. The site is located between two seams of development: a rugged mountainside forest on the eastern edge and densely settled residential neighborhoods on the western edge. Several small buildings remained from the original graceful layout of old farm buildings on the 120-acre site.

The process began with a visioning exercise and physical Master Plan to address both curricular and physical goals for the school. The resulting program defined 250,000 gross square feet of built space in the first phase of a complex build-out and an additional 100,000 gross square feet of future expansion, including a theater and natatorium.

Preservation of mature trees, old stone walls and several small historic buildings defined the layout hierarchy and site organization. The main entry sequence is organized by drop-off and parking along the wilderness edge, with distinct buildings organized around a central quadrangle. Defining this space are the Commons Building, Academics Center, Visual and Performing Arts Center and the Athletics Center. Playing and practice fields mediate between changing scales and context.

A contemporary expression, grounded in traditional planning roots, gives the new campus a striking sense of permanence and community. Throughout the day, as students move through the campus, distinct buildings with glass

The Ensworth School Nashville, Tennessee
2002–2004

rotundas and other entry forms serve as markers of discrete activity.

The Commons Building contains the library, dining hall and central administration. A dramatic two-story library, the physical and symbolic center of campus, is used for small group work, assemblies and individual study. Soaring two-story umbrella trusses are the focal point of the multipurpose dining space, which modulates between formal and informal configurations. The boundary between inside and outside, formal and informal, is further blurred with

Previous page Students gather in the courtyards and forecourts to the buildings at the center of campus. A slim campanile acts a vertical punctuation to the campus organization.

1 The campus is scaled to mediate between a mountainous, wild edge and a fine-grain residential neighborhood. Care was taken to preserve historic buildings and mature trees on the 120-acre site.
2 Buildings are sited to take advantage of the natural beauty and orientation of the landscape.
a Commons; **b** Academics; **c** theater and arts; **d** gymnasium; **e** stadium; **f** athletic fields

1

2

outdoor seating beyond the primarily glass facade facing the quadrangle. Spilling out onto the courtyard, students move to the Academics Center to the west, the Arts Center to the east, or the Athletics Center toward the south.

The Academics Center contains classrooms for the humanities, along with mathematics and state-of-the-art laboratories for chemistry, biology and physics. Unique collaborative spaces foster frequent interaction among students and faculty, including generous lounges, informal gathering areas and small group study spaces. In many classes, discussions take place around Harkness tables, where each student is actively involved in the learning process.

The Arts Center contains rehearsal space for dance, band, orchestra and other musical ensembles, a photography studio and darkroom, small theater for performances in the round, and spacious art studios. Multiple media are explored in the art studios, which feature flexible seating and working arrangements and an abundance of natural light. With a series of double doors to the outside, students often work in small groups along the

1

1/2 Seen from an interior quadrangle, the Commons Building brings the entire school together throughout the day. A contemporary school vernacular was chosen to respond to the existing lower school campus vocabulary and its future aspirations for building community.

2

1 A series of small moments between buildings breaks down the scale of distinct campus precincts.
2 As seen from the adjacent athletic fields, the clock tower is the heart of the interior campus organization.

arcade on the northern edge and a small courtyard to the northeast. The Athletics Center contains a flexible gymnasium with removable bleachers and a school-wide fitness center that is used by every student and athlete. The Athletics Center also acts as a forecourt to the playing fields, which are located below the main quadrangle.

The education of the entire person—mind, body and spirit—is exemplified in the mission of the school and its new physical expression. The arts and athletics are considered an integral part of each student's program, and the boundary

1 Small assemblies are often organized around a two-sided open fireplace on the second floor.
2 Taking advantage of the sequence of activity between buildings, an arcaded circulation links the Arts Center with the interior courtyard.
3 Fitness is a central part of the educational experience on campus.

Next page As visitors approach the campus, old stone walls and specimen trees line a curving drop-off to the main Commons Building. A southern vernacular of porches, colonnades and columns is blended with traditional New England roots.

Overleaf In the evening, the dining hall and terrace cast a warm glow across the heart of campus.

1

between these expressions, as well as the inside and outside, is intentionally porous. Small groups and classes often work in the courtyards and quadrangle. Anchored by the main circulation spine between buildings, which can be primarily external with the temperate Nashville climate, movement through the site is always linked to its extraordinary history and remarkable natural features.

Fast-track planning and implementation allowed the entire process, from Master Planning to occupancy, to be completed in just over two years. A significant accomplishment is that the entire project, including all site work and interior furnishings, was completed for just under $150 per square foot. ■

2

3

Two interventions on this venerable campus combine to remake the academic heart of the school. Two distinct architectural traditions create the primary character of campus. The original Gothic buildings by James Gamble Rogers and Bertram Goodhue evoke medieval, ecclesiastical and collegiate architecture. The site-specific inflection of the buildings extends their function and shape into the landscape, while the more recent "object" buildings are more static and less successful in creating a unified whole.

Celebrating this vocabulary as the integrating thread of the campus ensemble, the new buildings and renovations utilize similar form-making gestures, while acting as background to the established, historic buildings. The Gamble Rogers and Goodhue buildings provide the primary inspiration for the new Mathematics and Science Center. The building is broken down into humanly scaled elements and begins to create outdoor spaces, similar to the original buildings, using bays and dormers to interact with the landscape. A large courtyard acts as an outdoor classroom. A brutalist, 1960s library was enclosed in brick to create a cohesive assemblage of building skins.

The Science Center forms a new focal point on the campus edge where building and nature exist harmoniously. During early considerations of the campus as a whole, the importance of the pond at the campus center became apparent. A key issue of the new building intervention is its relationship to the water. The solution emphasizes the pond as the anchor for campus

Library, Mathematics and Science Building The Taft School, Watertown, Connecticut
1994–1997

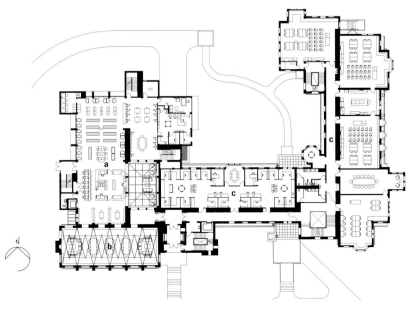

buildings. To emphasize water as a primary locus, the size of the pond was doubled, increasing its ability to physically engage the building edges.

During the preliminary investigation of campus hierarchy, the relationship of a modern intervention in the campus fabric came to the forefront. The 1960s-era library facade clashed dramatically with the ornamented campus aesthetic, and the interior spaces lacked many public amenities. As part of the larger campus reorganization, it was proposed to wrap the existing library facade and create a new reading room to continue the line of facades along the water's edge. Taken together, the new Mathematics and Science Center and expanded library create an educational center that presents a cohesive whole while unifying the renowned campus architecture.

Previous page The main stair circulation is animated by an illustrated history of science from the lever at the ground floor, to the computer chip at the top floor. **a** existing building; **b** new reading room; **c** science wing

1 Aerial view of the campus.
2 Lab areas are suffused with natural light.
3 The expanded campus pond with views of the new complex.

1

2

3

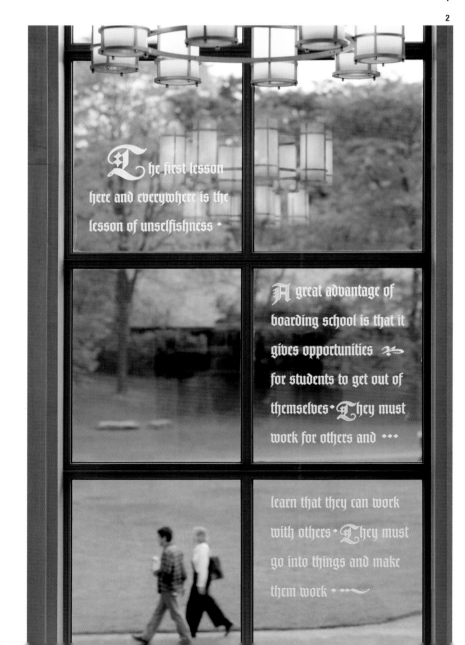

The new library construction consists of two large spaces and renovations to the existing building. The addition replaces the former sunken common area with a soaring great room.

Due to its internal configuration, the common room is organized by a skylight covering almost the entire ceiling. This space is the new heart of the library, an orientation point for students and the location of the new circulation desk.

Phrases from the school's founders are sandblasted in the glass of the library reading room, recalling the stained glass and etchings seen in the windows around campus and expressing the traditions and missions of the school. ■

1 The common room provides primary organization and library service.
2/3 Respecting the architectural traditions of campus, and recalling the founders' philosophy, the library windows frame student experiences.

Next page The main reading rooms now offer a place to gather, work and study.

1

2

The first lesson here and everywhere is the lesson of unselfishness ✦

A great advantage of boarding school is that it gives opportunities ✦ for students to get out of themselves ✦ They must work for others and ✦✦✦

learn that they can work with others ✦ They must go into things and make them work ✦✦✦

I TRUST THAT THE FUNDAMENTAL OF TRAINING, OF CHARACTER AND OF MIND TRAINING THE WHOLE PERSON WILL ALWAYS BE FOREMOST IN THE AMBITION OF THE SCHOOL.

3

This independent school campus is strongly integrated with its surrounding community. Several significant problems became apparent in the planning for new construction: an awkward drop-off and entry sequence to the school; the dangerous intersection of pedestrian and vehicular traffic; a lack of parking spaces for the student body; and the absence of appropriate landscaping on the campus green.

Through an evaluation of the circulation and layout of the campus, the goal was to improve/increase parking and improve access issues. One major concept was to create a new oval Campus Green as a means to unify campus buildings, improve wayfinding, and create a dramatic sense of arrival.

The challenge for this program was to bring science alive for young minds and foster a life-long relationship with the principles of scientific advancement. The program includes a 100-seat lecture room, six mathematics classrooms, seven laboratories, reading room, faculty work room, seminar room, two computer classrooms and an outdoor classroom.

The new Mathematics, Science and Technology Center transforms teaching at the secondary school level. The solution maximizes natural daylighting, allows for easy supervision, and provides many areas for students and faculty to coexist outside the classroom to foster learning through collaboration— both casual and formal. Siting the new building on the northwest edge of

The Fannie Cox Center for Science, Math and Technology

Friends' Central School Wynnewood, Pennsylvania
2001–2003

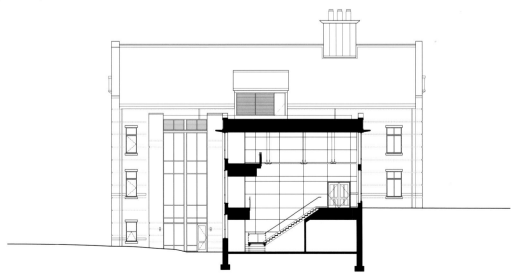

Previous page The highly transparent entry form is located between two traditional gabled elements.

1 The exterior courtyard features a relief map of the Delaware River basin, which comes alive when the river and its tributaries flow with rainwater. It has become a central meeting place and teaching tool for the entire campus.

2 The science center creates an entirely new vehicular and pedestrian campus circulation, while preserving major specimen trees.

Next page The lobby is a meeting place for students and a new front door for the sciences.

the campus strengthens the internal campus green and takes advantage of the interesting topography of the site as a way to mitigate scale and open up views to the landscape beyond. The building location takes advantage of existing steep grades on the campus, and complements the architecture of a Gothic stone mansion, a formative icon on campus. The boundaries between inside and outside learning spaces are intentionally blurred. In collaboration with the artist Stacy Levy, the team developed an outdoor classroom that celebrates the ecological framework of the local rivershed system. ■

1

2

This private boarding school was founded in 1810 and renamed Lawrenceville in 1883. At the time of its renaming, the school engaged the famed landscape architect Frederick Law Olmsted to help bring order to the campus and reflect its noble ideals. Olmsted devised the Circle as the formative and spiritual heart of campus. The Circle is now a designated national landmark and the design of Lawrenceville's beautiful campus is primarily credited to Olmsted's strong ordering principles.

The John Dixon Library was designed by Delano and Aldrich, a classicist architectural practice, and completed in 1931. The building holds important historical significance, not only as one of the five remaining Delano and Aldrich buildings in the country, but also because of its prominent location on campus.

The challenge of this commission was to renovate the original Dixon Library and addition, and also define a new facility to house the growing needs of the Art Department. As the campus expanded over the previous 40 years, the Art Department scattered into multiple buildings, often relegated to basement rooms and other periphery spaces. After the completion of a new library located on another part of campus, the existing Dixon Library was renovated and expanded to house the school's first Visual Arts Center.

Sited at the seam between the school's two architectural vernaculars—the intellectual (classical)

Visual Arts Building and Library Lawrenceville School, Lawrenceville, New Jersey
1994–1998

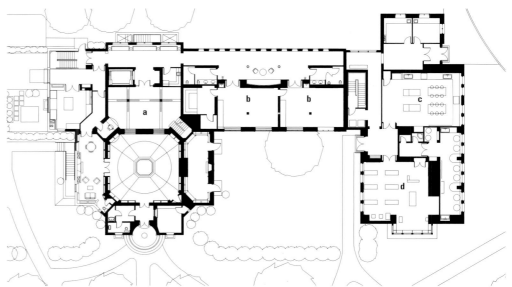

Previous pages The double-height studios are flexible for many different teaching styles and disciplines. **a** existing building; **b** foundations studio; **c** wood shop; **d** graphics studio

1 Brick piers continue the masonry cornice line of surrounding buildings, while a zinc roof and large punched openings evoke a new openness to the campus. **2** A zinc-clad bay in the new visual arts center responds to the entrance portico of the historic Dixon Library.

Next page A warm-toned brick complements the predominant campus vocabulary.

1

2

and the spiritual (romantic)—the building bridges the Olmsted and Delano sections of the campus and re-establishes equilibrium for the campus. The legacy of a profound cultural and historic memory informed the project from the outset and dictated a solution that bridges the old and new traditions in a respectful manner.

Achieving this delicate balance within the diverse campus context, the building recalls similar forms of the Dixon Library, realized in new and modern materials. Rich wood millwork

in the existing library acts as a dramatic backdrop to a gallery of diverse artworks.

The new construction is bridged through a renovated corridor featuring places to gather, draw or reflect. The corridor also acts as an additional gallery space.

Double-height drawing and painting studios are flooded with natural light, and together with expanded classrooms and meeting areas, pronounce the renewed importance of the arts at Lawrenceville. ■

1 Library interiors feature both fixed and moveable furnishings.
2 Reading and lounge areas overlook an active campus thoroughfare.

Next page The scale of the library facade is broken down by the use of dormers, bays and punched openings. Distinct materials take their cue from the surrounding mix of Romantic architecture.

1

2

After a major fire destroyed their 30-year-old facility in January of 1994, the largest Orthodox congregation in the Boston area immediately began the task of rebuilding. The goal was to rebuild on the same site while increasing the facility size by 25 percent.

Nestled into the dense residential fabric of the neighborhood, the new structure needed to both fit in with its neighbors and also be a recognizable landmark. Driving the building's layout was the traditional Halacha law, which required the eastern orientation of both the sanctuary and the chapel so members may pray facing Jerusalem. This presented a particular challenge due to site setback constraints and the need to angle these pieces off the prevailing street grid.

The program called for a Bet Knesset (main sanctuary) seating more than 500 people, a Bet Medrash (chapel) to provide for daily services and to serve as a study hall and library, a social hall, and support facilities including administrative offices and three classrooms.

The interior palette of materials includes maple panels, Jerusalem stone and the sculptural use of light. The main lobby, with extensive millwork details, including Hebrew inscriptions over the doors to the main rooms and ceremonial washing sink area, is a central focus of the building. During the day, the lobby is bathed with natural light from a grand skylight in the roof penetrating the building through a large sculpted opening in the second floor.

A panoramic window overlooking the social hall from the second-floor lobby provides further means for natural light to reach into the interior spaces of the building. The balcony creates views into

Young Israel Synagogue Brookline, Massachusetts
1994–1996

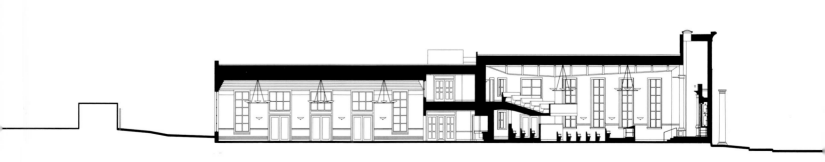

the social hall and provides a bird's-eye view for video and still photography of social events.

In the sanctuary, 12 large windows allow light to filter into the room while screening activity from the street through the creative use of inset prisms. Throughout all times of the day, the room is activated with light and shadow.

Numerous main sanctuary layouts were investigated with the congregation, including the Halachic issue requiring the separation of men's and women's seating. A resulting consensus design provides for the majority of women's seating in a low balcony or gallery section, an unusual solution for a traditional congregation. To provide the required visual separation between men and women, a unique Mechitzah or screen wall is constructed of millwork elements and sandblasted

Previous page The main sanctuary comfortably accommodates men and women on two levels.

1 Ground floor plan
2 Articulation of the building elements reflects the religious tradition of orienting toward Jerusalem, while recalling the fractured nature of the city's architectural history.

1

1 Light dances in the sanctuary throughout the day.
2 The small chapel provides a place for the integration of prayer and learning.

Next page The entry lobby is punctuated by a skylight, suffusing the natural palette of materials with light.

Hebrew letters carved out of acrylic panels, with text from the first three verses of *Eishet Chayil*.

Behind the Mechitzah, the balance of the seating is on a raised platform on the ground floor with sculpted ceilings overhead. All of the women's seating in the main sanctuary, including the furthest seat in the upper corners of the balcony, is closer to the Ark than any of the seats in the women's section of the old shul. ■

1

2

The existing perform-ing arts theater on this southern university cam-pus housed a non-profit professional repertory company and the graduate programs of the university in a triangularly shaped box-like structure. The facility was inadequate for both the growing enrollments in the theater disciplines and the com-pany's needs. Additionally, department functions were scattered in six buildings across the campus.

Although a major gateway into this precinct of the campus, the existing building was recessed from the street. Since depart-ment functions were also scattered throughout multiple buildings, the drama department lacked an identifiable presence. A lack of departmen-tal consolidation also

severely limited interaction between students, faculty and staff members, and restricted undergraduate student exposure to the professional theater.

The challenge was to bring together the entire pro-gram, including teaching, rehearsal and perfor-mance, in an economical solution that establishes a strong identity for the university.

An addition to the theater features a curving colon-nade with a glass clerestory and creates a new identity for the entire department. The form of the addition minimizes the sharp-edged facade of the existing theater building and acts as a forecourt to the per-formance theater within. Its sweeping form also engages the street edge, creating a new major entry

Center for Dramatic Arts University of North Carolina, Chapel Hill, North Carolina
1996–1999

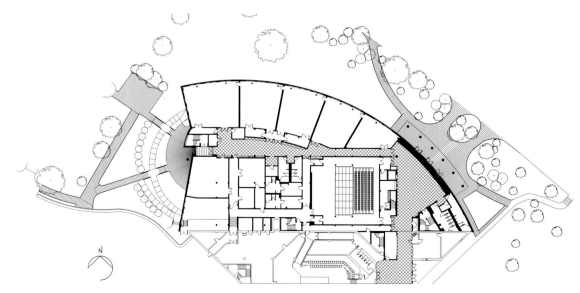

sequence onto campus. The curving form of the addition also helps to marry the odd geometry of the triangularly shaped building into the grid of the campus. A warm brick was selected to complement the material vocabulary of the campus, together with an abundance of glass to animate the site at night when most performances take place.

The university was fortunate to have a professional local repertory company in residence, allowing for the addition to be organized

Previous page The colonnade is a welcome front door to the theater arts.

1 Removable railings and seating offer flexibility for teaching and performance.
2 Diagram of performance seating configurations in the black box theater.

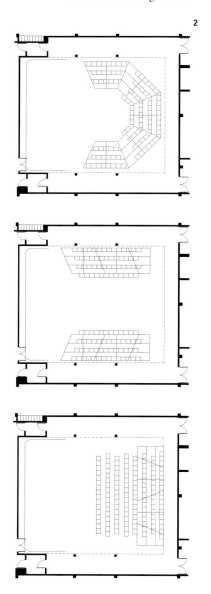

1 The clerestory creates an open feeling in faculty offices.
2 A warm palette of maple and stone acts as a neutral backdrop for large-scale gathering.

with the teaching and rehearsal components together. As a result, the main performance theater remained in the existing building and the teaching/rehearsal theater in the addition was designed as a flexible black box. A variety of flexible seating arrangements allows for both the company rehearsal needs and the university's teaching needs.

At the second level, the clerestory brings light into the upper band of offices and studios, offers views out to a protected forested area, and gives the visitor a sense of being nestled into a wooded environment.

The unified functions of the existing theater and new building allow teaching, rehearsal and performance elements to

1

act synergistically between the university and the professional company, giving students a valuable exposure to the profession. With all departmental functions as well as professional performance needs provided for, including the costume/wardrobe operations, paint/scene shops, and studios for movement, voice and acting practice, the new facility is truly a unified workshop for discovery rather than a dry academic space.

This exploration into blurring the boundaries between academic training and professional exposure has dramatically raised the profile of the university's graduate program in the theater arts. ▮

1 At night, when most performances take place, the transparent lobby animates the main sequence through campus.

1

Celebration is Disney's concept for the creation of an American small town. The Master Plan for the entire town envisioned a series of landmarks or meeting nodes to organize the sequence through its streets, including a cinema, bank and an inn.

Inspired by noted 1920s Florida wood-frame vernacular, the 115-room Inn complements the town's overall character, without overwhelming its scale and detail. To break down the scale, massing is organized by three primary elements: a main house, garden wing and west wing. The arrival sequence is characterized by a gracious brick motor court, with a transparent lobby element that offers glimpses of the pool and lake beyond the front doors.

The additive quality of the building form reflects multiple room experiences: garden rooms, tower suites, lake-view rooms and dormer rooms. It also echoes the actual history of many small-town inns, which grew from landmark houses over time. Design elements associated with older, landmark homes in resort areas include dormers, balconies, awnings and substantial roof overhangs.

On the horizon, the Inn functions as a pivotal landmark within Celebration, with a tower that is a visual focal point from anywhere within the town. The symmetrical and axial nature of its facade recognizes the importance of its site along the lake and its overall composition within the community.

The neutral palette of color also reinforces the sense of the Inn being settled into the landscape. Lush

Inn at Celebration Celebration, Florida
1999–2001

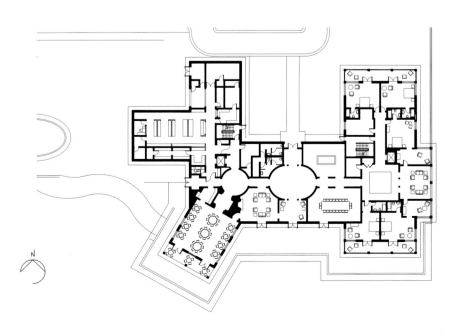

native plantings which surround the Inn are also brought to the foreground with the restrained use of exterior materials.

The distinctly residential character of the Inn evokes the grand traditions of waterfront building, while reinforcing the themes of small town and home. ▪

Previous page A series of towers and lanterns defines the Inn from within the town of Celebration.

1 Main entry into the Inn features a comfortable street-level experience.
2 From the lake, the Inn is well integrated into the landscape.

Next page The scale and character are in keeping with the overall community fabric.

1

2

The 81 residential units comprising the Crossings at WaterSound Beach are distributed across a spectacular coastal site in four individual buildings. Each grouping is linked by a series of small-scale bridges that creates a strong sequence through the landscape. Each grouping has a distinct yet interrelated identity, characterized by entries that express an attention to the scale of the individual.

Drawing inspiration from historic coastal summer homes of the Northeast, the buildings are evocative of a simpler, more casual time. The soaring curved roof lines mimic the dune landscape and provide a recognizable and distinguished profile on the horizon. Other elements are borrowed from familiar historic examples reinterpreted in a contemporary manner. ■

Next page A series of wooden bridges connect diverse natural landscapes through the site.

WaterSound Bridges WaterSound, Florida
1999–2003

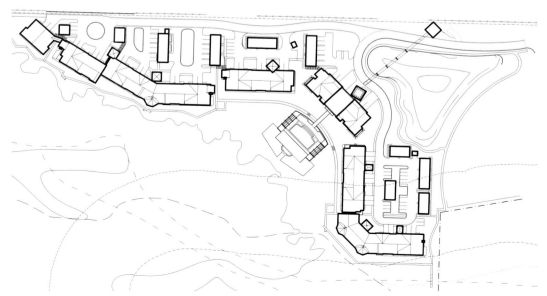

The town of Gambier and Kenyon College are intimately linked. The majority of academic buildings are located within the college's historic core, while administrative/ student services and housing are carefully integrated in the town's residential fabric.

When planning a new administrative office in the quiet northwest corner of the campus, an intentional residential character that evokes the surrounding rural vernacular was adopted. Along the street edge, the rhythm, scale and proportion of facades create an ensemble that honors the balance between college and village.

Two wood-framed elements are linked by an enclosed connector with a rotunda at its center. Simple metal roofs, articulated with stair towers and shed dormers, create an intimate-scale transition between the amount of facade perceived at the ground plane and the distant views of the roof plane at street level.

The symmetrical buildings contain administrative offices with generous reception and lounge areas. The rotunda contains common spaces, including a kitchen, dining area, lounge and a conference center module. Large groupings of residential-scaled window openings exploit the small scale of the forms, while also distinguishing its distinct academic functions.

Light and transparent details, including wood clapboard siding and trimmed window

Eaton Center Kenyon College, Gambier, Ohio
1997–2000

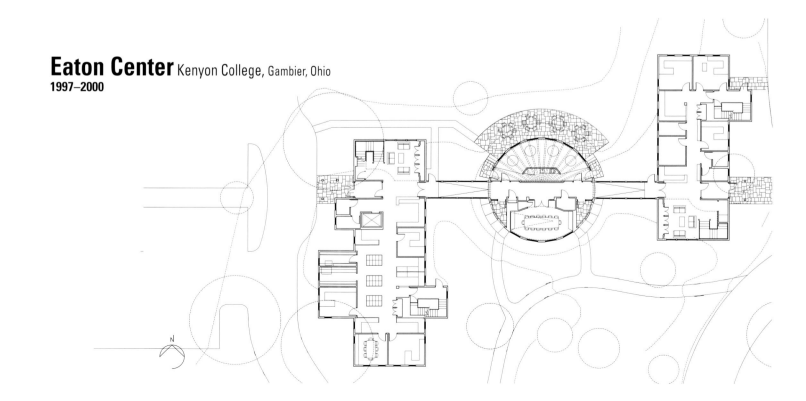

openings, together with long open connectors, balance the generous roof forms while preserving and enhancing the mature landscape. The collage of building forms frames pristine views across the site.

Taken together, the complex contributes to a collaborative working environment, appropriately scaled to its residential neighbors. ■

Previous page The conference center is located in the rotunda between the main house forms.

1 An interior lounge is also in keeping with the residential character of the building elements.
2 A single-story connector knits together the main building volumes.

One of the central questions being asked by college and university administrators is how to deal with the vast stock of outmoded and failing 1960s-era buildings. When the firm was engaged by the University of New Hampshire to analyze its main library, built in 1957 and expanded in 1967, student visits were at an all-time low. The original library was designed with a traditional separation between the public areas, service and stacks. With its expansion 10 years later, large floor plates further eroded the definition between the public use areas and stacks. While the university's Sputnik-era library provided 170,000 square feet of space, its organization was mainly for the storage of books. Adding to this dilemma was the drab character and quality of interior finishes. Low ceilings of acoustical tile panels and striped carpet, which covered floors and ran up interior walls and across public service desks, created a dark and convoluted public circulation.

The simplicity of traditional New England forms and reuse of building structure characterizes the design solution. With a limited public university construction budget, the approach was to reuse the existing building for stacks, reference areas and staff, together with new construction that contains large public reading areas and primary library service. A 45,000-square-foot addition on the north and east edges of the building comprise the

Dimond Library University of New Hampshire, Durham, New Hampshire
1994–1998

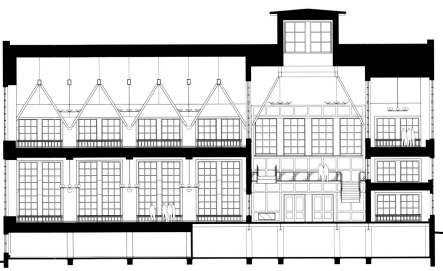

Previous page The main reading room recalls the grand public spaces of turn-of-the-century libraries and also makes a new home for student interaction on campus.

1 A three-story lobby creates a welcome first experience into the library. Student visits to the library doubled in its first year of operation.
2 The lantern-like light well above the grand entry stair leads to the second-floor reading room.

Next page 1 The main entrance now engages with the primary campus circulation, creating a strong courtyard organization.
2 Site plan

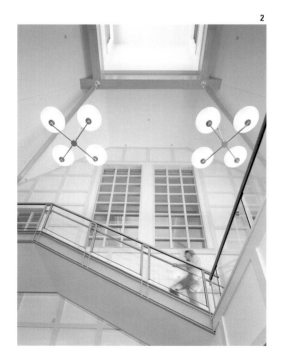

2

new reading rooms, while the existing structure was renovated and functionally reorganized. The existing building was set back from the center of the most significant campus quadrangle, creating a dark and forbidding entry sequence. Taking down the old entry portico and covering two sides of the existing building with taller new construction allowed the building forms to be reinserted into the main campus organization with a more civic-scaled presence. Two new wings that house the major public spaces of the library are brought out further into the primary central courtyard on campus to better engage the student pedestrian experience. The north wing fronts and completes the central courtyard of the campus. The east wing opens to vistas across the rolling New England setting. At night, the tall reading rooms behind the oversized windows

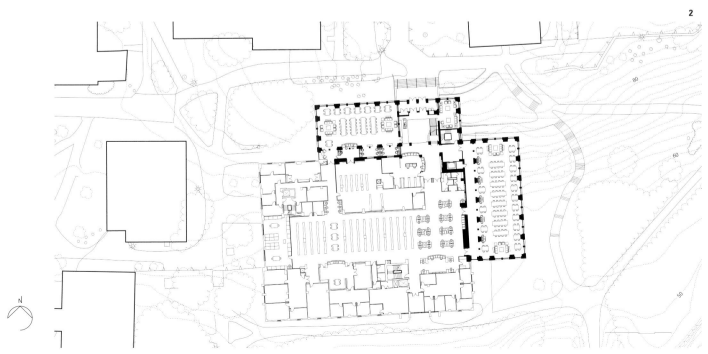

are illuminated, casting light across the courtyard and campus, and inviting students within.

In the old sections of the building, all interior finishes were replaced and the location of interior partitions and finishes were replanned for better efficiency. Throughout the six levels, the 210,000-square-foot floor plate is organized for consistency as well as efficiency. The library visitor is oriented on each floor with reference to the three-story entrance lobby and can proceed to the reading rooms, stacks or the staff/service points without hesitation. ■

1 Reading rooms feature wired ports at large tables and a variety of lounge and soft seating.
2 A special collections area on the lower level takes advantage of steep grade changes.

Next page The simplicity of the gabled roof form expresses the double-height volume of the public reading rooms.

1

2

This pristine liberal arts college campus features a collection of primarily Gothic buildings, modeled after European churches and colleges. The original campus plan is centered on a mile-long walk lined with stately buildings that refer to the Gothic, Romanesque and Neoclassical traditions. In the last major campus expansion of the 1960s and 70s, several buildings that clashed with tradition were erected on the campus, including a chemistry building that blocked the main artery to the campus.

The original program called for a single new structure to house the sciences. In a departure, the solution suggested demolition of a 1962 chemistry building, together with an additional 75,000 square feet of new construction and renovation and replanning of the rest of the sciences complex in existing buildings to form a new sciences quadrangle that rebalances the rhythm of buildings and open space in this part of the campus.

The interdisciplinary nature of science today prescribes interconnections, both physical and programmatic, between different disciplines. Connecting the new science facilities to the existing 1968 biology building, and placing a state-of-the-art science complex into an historic campus proved to be an interesting challenge in terms of campus planning and programming.

The two new science complex buildings, housing chemistry and math/physics, are connected to each other and the existing biology building via glass-

Mathematics and Science Complex Kenyon College, Gambier, Ohio
1997–2001

Previous page The complex knits together old and new, traditional and modern, open and closed.

1 A dynamic tension between solid and void is seen in the fenestration. **2** Ground floor plan of the complex illustrates the connection between buildings. **a** psychology building (renovated); **b** biology building (addition and renovation); **c** chemistry building (new); **d** physics building (new)

Next page The connection between circulation paths of the buildings continues on the upper levels of the complex.

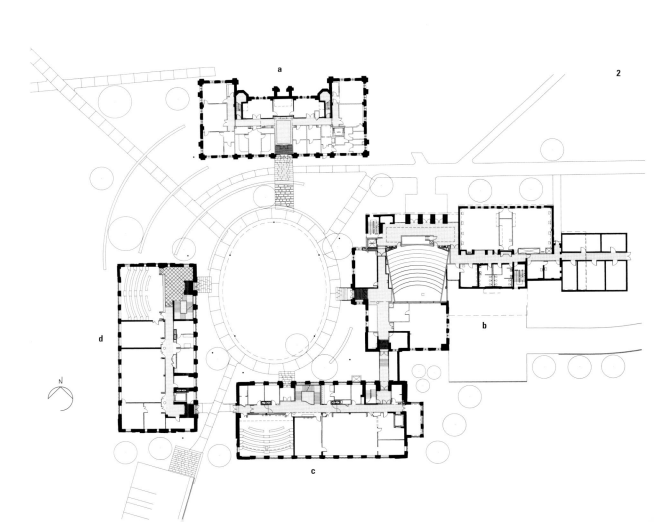

1

2

1

enclosed bridges and underground passages. The fourth science building, the historic Mather Hall, was renovated to house psychology. The academic Gothic-style building informs the aesthetics of the new chemistry, and math/physics buildings, and the biology addition. It also completes the new science quadrangle, which is both the physical and symbolic heart of the science complex.

The quadrangle of small buildings is more in scale with the historic architecture of the campus. To respect the tension between nature and buildings, the interiors are light and airy, with white limestone floors, wide curved stairwells, and study rooms with floor-to-ceiling windows. The exterior facades are united by the use of sandstone from the same quarry.

The new laboratory spaces are based on a modular design that enables the school to expand, contract and renovate a laboratory space without interrupting the use of other laboratories in the building. The flexibility of this modular design creates long-term adaptability for both pedagogical and scientific advances. ■

1/2 Stairwells are animated by overscaled windows. Glass prisms are embedded in the fenestration, creating changing patterns throughout the day.

Next page 1 A chemistry laboratory features a flexible module for changing teaching and research needs.
2 A raised tier lecture hall is shared between departments.
3 As seen in the upper-level plan, interior partitions can be easily reconfigured with a column-free structure.

Overleaf The new buildings feature the same Briar Hill stone, with larger metal-clad bays and wider openings. The scale and complementary use of materials creates a comfortable fit between the old and new buildings.

2

1

2

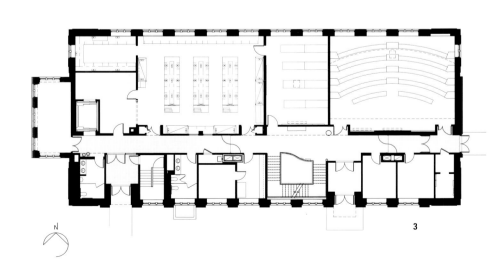

3

This picturesque New England private school campus has a proud 200-year history. The campus grew slowly and deliberately over time, yet a close examination of current campus patterns revealed that the core of the academic experience had begun to erode. The rapid expansion of technological and scientific progress and concomitant pedagogical shift necessitated a complete reimagining of the sciences' presence on campus.

The opportunity to create a long-term underpinning for campus development is at the heart of the siting solution. The new building, set among athletic fields and adjacent to an 18th-century Gothic building, forms a new campus geometry by creating two connected quadrangles. This new order links to the campus'

main quadrangle, with its historic structures, in a larger scale appropriate to its function. To balance the mass of the buildings, a significant framing of open space is established. Future buildings are also planned to maintain a cohesive rhythm of solid and void.

A light, buff-colored brick, with cast accents and metal details, complements the main campus vocabulary of materials. Traditional New England forms are exploited, including gabled roofs, projecting bays, and mill-like chimneys that contain the required mechanical penetrations of modern science teaching and research. Fenestration combines both smaller punched openings and large expanses of double-height glass in main circulation and high occupancy spaces. Laboratories are flooded with natural light,

Jeppesen Science Center Berwick Academy, South Berwick, Maine
1998–1999

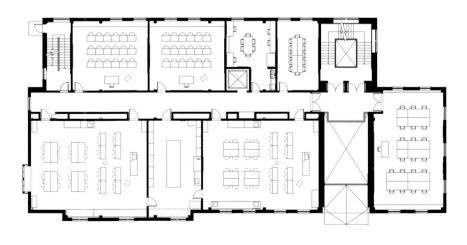

creating a comfortable environment for the first, formative introduction to the sciences.

The building houses science programs for all 13 grades, mathematics classes for the Upper School, and core technology programs for the entire school. ■

Previous page As the building turns the corner of the quad, circulation is celebrated, inviting all students to participate in the discovery of science.

1 A traditional gable roof is in keeping with views toward the western edge of campus
2 A smaller teaching laboratory
3 Primary elevation across the new quadrangle

Next page Stair corridors create a crossroads for movement through the building and a special place for interaction.

1

2

3

This independent school was founded in 1791 to promote "virtue and useful knowledge among the rising generations." For more than 200 years, the Academy has pursued its mission through a classical education of the whole person.

A multi-phased comprehensive Master Plan called for significant expansion of campus facilities and reorganization of the interior heart of the campus fabric. A primary tenet was the creation of a campus oval to organize the academic core buildings into two connected quadrangles. In the first phase, two new buildings, a mathematics and science center and a library, form the dominant end of the quadrangle and express a

larger scale and formality to anchor an elevated sense of place. A buff-colored brick, with precast and copper accents, is used appropriately to meld with historical precedents on campus. Strong gabled roof forms with a lantern-like tower create a locus for orientation across campus.

The 25,000-square-foot library supports all age groups of the school, with programmed spaces for a two-story reading room, an archives suite, multiple study rooms, library staff areas, a seminar room, art gallery, computer classroom and a Lower School classroom serving grades K–4.

A graphic of the history of the written word complements the visitor sequence

Jackson Library Berwick Academy, South Berwick, Maine
2000–2002

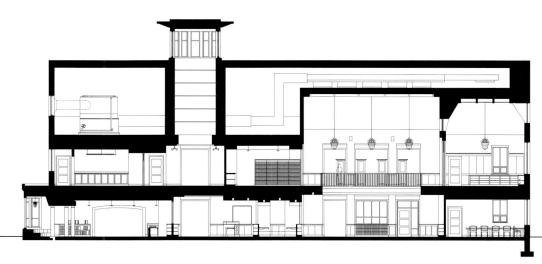

Previous page The new library fronts and completes the main campus quadrangle.

1 Detail of entry level graphics
2 The library reading room on the second level is animated by quotations from noted authors and philosophers.

throughout the building, beginning at the main entrance and culminating in the reading room. Early cuneiforms and alphabets are integrated into the front door and lobby area, and follow a progression through the main circulation. In the contemplative two-story reading room, a graphic frieze with quotations from great authors throughout history completes the physical and intellectual journey. ■

1

Kenyon College is one of the nation's finest liberal arts colleges, located on an Ohio hilltop of exceptional beauty. The heart of the campus is a collection of Collegiate Gothic buildings, knitted together with several Neoclassical structures. An ambitious campus transformation, comprised of an addition to the music building and the creation of a new biology and chemistry complex, restores a formal quadrangle around a green oval. This reorganization of the interior academic core redefines a new campus edge, strengthens a sense of place and fosters the spirit of community.

The primary challenge was to replicate the scale of the original Neoclassical Rosse Hall with an addition sympathetic in material and form. Simplicity of materials and gestures in the new addition supports the idea of a background building in the new campus organization.

The new 14,000-square-foot addition of Storer Hall includes a recording studio, green room, electronic music laboratories, band room, 136-seat recital hall, and a collection of teaching, rehearsal and office space. Each teacher's office can accommodate a grand piano and doubles as a private teaching area for lessons and small group sessions. This concept carries throughout the interior, as a grand piano can be on any floor, in any of the interior rooms. The elevator is large enough to accommodate the movement of all types of instruments.

A single monumental column marks the new entrance to the music department from the campus green. Through a series of

Music Building Kenyon College, Gambier, Ohio
1997–2000

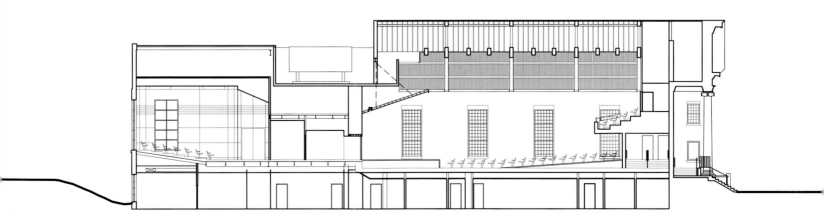

1

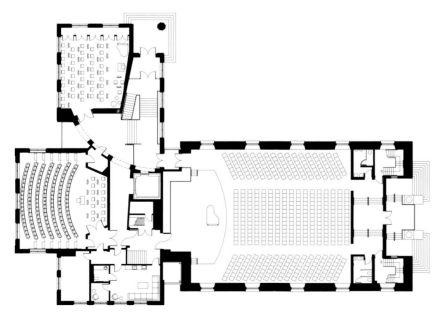

2

design investigations for an appropriate language for this element, the column evolved into an abstracted interpretation of historic precedents.

Complementary large-scale window openings in Storer Hall recall the formal fenestration of Rosse Hall. These double-height windows offer views out onto the campus green and bring light into the main recital hall. The scale of fenestration also brings light into all levels of the addition, including the lower-level rehearsal rooms, which are more typically carved out of interstitial and basement-level spaces. A fine-grain brick with cast stone trim adds texture and interest to the sandstone material of the existing building.

Previous page The simplicity of form is in deference to the Neoclassical composition of Rosse Hall.

1 A three-story lobby washes the interior circulation with light and offers remarkable views onto the main campus.
2 Ground level plan

Next page The main stair acts as a gathering place and forecourt to both the concert hall and new recital hall.

N

1 A 136-seat recital hall is finished with a warm-toned maple paneling. An ebony line frieze at the window height recalls musical notation.
2 Large interior openings look onto the stairwell and allow borrowed light to activate the circulation.

Primary circulation is organized by a three-story lobby, which can be used in a variety of ways including receptions, performances, gathering space and circulation. The main stair, generously scaled and filled with light, connects activities on all three levels. The renovation and new construction form a cohesive whole and create a new heart for the music program. ■

1

2

Inspired by both modern movement elements and the expression of structure in Chicago architecture, this mixed-use arts center marks a new civic destination for the city's North Shore. The existing site contained remnants of urban renewal efforts, including a large-scale hotel, commercial properties and difficult surface and structured parking. This cacophony of influences led to the decision to use transparency as a way to announce and celebrate arrival.

The grand facade is oriented to be seen from the main boulevard and features two-story columns that support a translucent canopy structure. The continuous colonnade and glass wall with cornice is set back from the street to accommodate abutting owners of the streetside parcel. At night, the two-story lobby glows with welcoming activity and its grand curving stairs and balconies allow the theatergoers themselves to animate the facade.

Program elements in the 68,000-square-foot facility include an 840-seat theater with full 70-foot fly loft, dressing rooms and support spaces, and a large multi-purpose room that provides independent, flexible space. The smaller space can be configured to seat up to 350 in a theater arena or 500 in a sit-down dinner. Each of the two theater spaces contain separate entries, lobbies, restrooms and support spaces. The box office is at the hub of the building, serving both theaters.

The 840-seat main theater features a single balcony that sweeps around toward the proscenium. The curves of the front facade

North Shore Center for the Performing Arts Skokie, Illinois
1993–1996

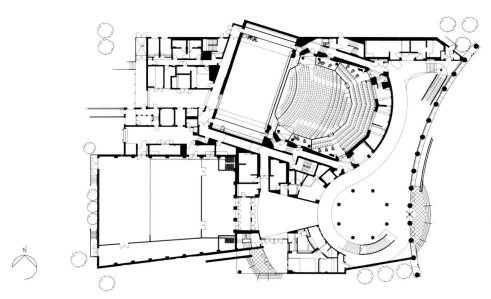

are continued in the interior lobbies and theater. The theater offers a warm intimacy, with the furthest seat only 56 feet from the stage.

The Northlight Theatre, seating approximately 350 people, is an amphitheater-style setting used primarily for drama performances. A thrust stage is accessed by vomitories with steeply raked seats to provide excellent sightlines for the audience. ■

Previous page The exterior canopy presents a new civic face to this downtown district.

1 The main theater utilizes maple tier fronts, shaped concrete walls and acoustical clouds to amplify and control sound.
2 The flexible smaller theater can be converted to a flat-floor reception area by collapsing the tiered seating.

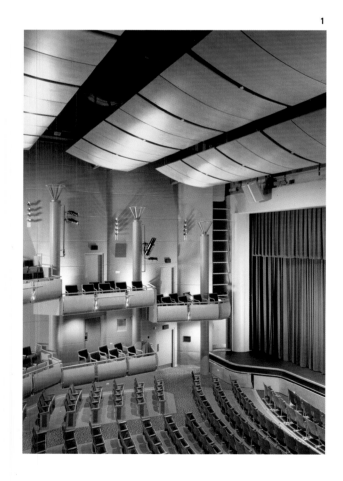

To create a truly flexible container to support a thriving arts program, as well as create a destination for the entire student body as an assembly space, the program for this new arts center includes a highly adaptable 460-seat main theater, a 125-seat workshop theater, and supporting spaces for the school's curricular mission.

A consistency of masonry materials and a strong organizational device in the main campus oval (designed by Frederick Law Olmsted) contribute to the formal character of the campus. In order to mediate scale, the building was sited to include a new entry road on the eastern edge and formal gates into the core of the campus fabric. A gently curving lobby form utilizes an expansive plane of glass, supported by masonry piers. A lantern-like tower closest to the main pedestrian path beckons the student body into the arts experience.

Since the program is experientially based, all of the spaces are designed for multiple uses. The main theater may be configured in a variety of experimental configurations. A 20- x 40-foot proscenium, with proportions of a dance theater, is supported by a forestage that can thrust 14 feet beyond the proscenium. Seats in the first two rows are removable to allow flexible staging. Differing levels of pit fillers can be added, allowing the users to move almost one-third of the way into the orchestra level. Additionally, the side boxes flow into the stage and project into the audience. This allows the edges to double as stage area and also facilitates access. Removable railings are used

Campbell Center for the Performing Arts The Groton School, Groton, Massachussets
2002–2005

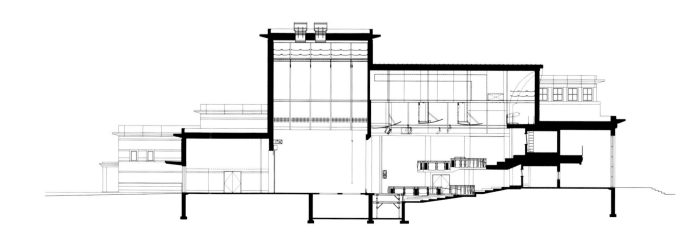

in both the pit and side boxes. A deep stage, with the scene shop to the rear, facilitates moving large sets and installations.

Underscoring the primacy of the student experience, the interior spaces create an intimate and supportive learning environment. Acoustics in the main theater are tuned so students do not have to be amplified, with the goal of building confidence in the presentation role. The shallow fan-shaped seating arrangement, where the furthest seat in both the orchestra and balcony are only 40 feet from the stage, also helps the audience and performer become intimately connected. With a foreshortened two-story balcony, the house feels full in a variety of configurations.

A workshop theater, seating 80-125, depending on how it is used, supports the main theater. A full control room, resilient performance floor, and suspended pipe system with full catwalk access allows

Previous page Simple brick patterning and oversized columns help to break down the scale of the arts center and mediate with more intimate adjacent buildings.

1 The main theater features acoustics tuned for experimentation and learning. The clouds help amplify the spoken word, and combined with the seating configuration, help to build confidence for the new performer.

Next page New pedestrian pathways which wrap along the front elevation knit together the historic and new precincts of campus.

2 Ground level plan
3 Interior of the lantern-like tower is activated by its transparent nature.

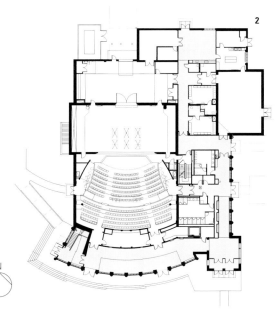

students to create multiple environments. Throughout the theaters, catwalks and ladders are designed with strong safety considerations to ensure student participation and learning. The tension between formal and informal, fixed and flexible, technical and creative, serves as a strong teaching device for students' first, formative theater experience. ■

2

This steeply sloping New England college campus is traditionally viewed from a distance, and as the college grew, its profile of buildings on the horizon was distinguished by a series of ornamental towers and rooflines. The challenge of this commission was to knit together two elevations of the steep campus with a new classroom and library building in its center, while also enunciating its function on the hill.

The plan and aesthetic for the building resulted from several important concepts. On a visceral level, the site is at the physical and intellectual heart of the campus. From a campus planning point of view, the building acts as both a lateral and vertical crossroads for students, faculty, staff and visitors to move through the campus. The new building's loca-tion at the center of its 174-acre setting is a critical part of the intended goal of providing space for so-cial dialogue and community interface. Connecting the upper and lower elevations of the campus, which is primarily traversed by foot, was a key determinant in the plan layout.

The seven-story building is organized with three stories rising above the hill and four stories descending down the hill. Entrances to the building are found both at the lower courtyard level (level one in plan) and the upper campus elevation (level three), the primary entrance for students attending classes in the building. This vital connection links the lower half of the campus, where academic life prevails, with the upper half of the campus, the location of

Carol and Park B. Smith Hall College of the Holy Cross, Worcester, Massachusetts
1998–2001

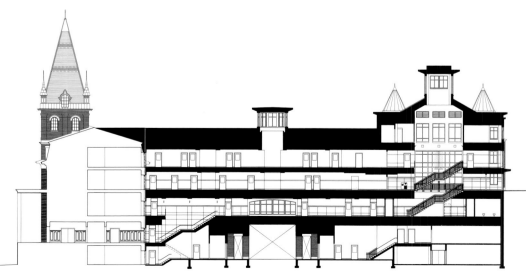

CAROL & PARK B. SMITH HALL

Previous page The lower level is conceived as a piazza/garden courtyard.

1 Forms respond to both historic and contemporary influences.
2 A warm-toned brick with wood and stone accents harmonizes with the predominant campus materials.

Next page The main entrance knits together the upper and lower precincts of campus.

1

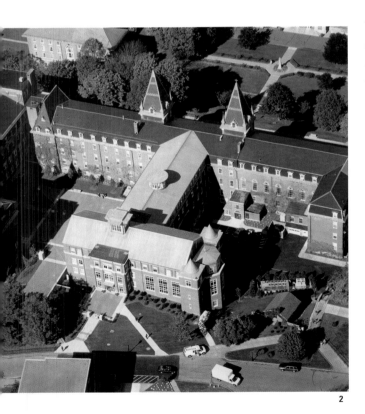

2

the residence halls and the focus of most of the college's social life.

With important elevations on both the front and rear and no obvious back to the building, the solution succeeds by extending the historic fabric of the campus. It provides views to the traditional quadrangles of the campus while creating new courtyards with other neighboring, historic buildings conceptualized as Italian gardens. The form-making reinforces the campus history by paying homage to beloved landmarks including a cemetery, a chapel and an historic bakery. The choice of a richly toned and variegated brick, with stone and metal accents, harmonizes with the lan-

guage of adjacent historic buildings.

The goals for the building design included establishing a contemplative spirit to preside over the space, as well as the programs offered within. The physical space needed to be flexible, and provide a space for quiet meditation as well as for intellectual stimulation through discussion. The center serves to integrate all the departments and groups that were previously dispersed throughout campus. The center facilitates the collaboration of efforts among academic departments, groups and events and provides a central meeting place on campus for a wide variety of seminars, workshops and discussions for stu-

1 The composition of recognizable towers on the skyline is enhanced with new forms.
2 First level plan

Next page The scale of the library/chapel windows offer spectacular views between the upper and lower campuses. It is a place for reflection, study, celebration and discussion.

Overleaf The custom translucent glass installation transforms in changing light.

dents of all faiths, as well as the entire surrounding community. The center is a premier example of merging a liberal arts education with spirituality.

1

Connections between the upper and lower halves of the campus are intentionally enmeshed, with multiple entrances and exterior punctuations in the building. The building acts as a crossroads between precincts on campus: academic and residential, social and formal, upper and lower, traditional and modern. ▪

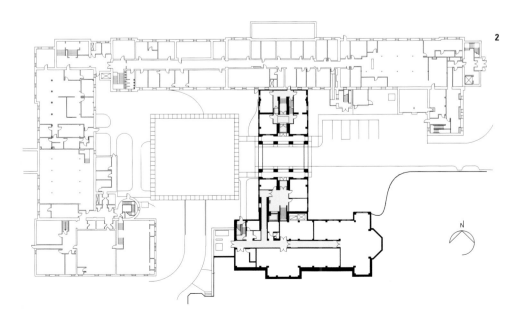

2

This picturesque college campus on the ridge of rolling hills in central Ohio was seriously in need of additional academic space. With few obvious building sites in the campus core, the challenge was to accommodate more than 100,000 gross square feet of new facilities in the neighborhood of the academic quadrangle with minimum disruption to its community and academic schedule. The first step in the process was to update and repair the compromises and deficiencies that had accrued since the Olmsted brothers produced their Master Plan early in the 20th century.

An outdated 1960s science building and a student center that had lost much of its luster marked the northern boundary of the campus core. Parking, service access and dumpsters filled the space behind the buildings before the start of the steep slope toward the fields below.

The new Master Plan reinforces the rhythm and integrity of individual quads as the primary orientation of the campus. It also recommends a functional reorganization and expansion of campus circulation to strengthen the internal fabric of campus. The solution suggests the placement of a new 380-car underground parking garage against the north slope of the College Hill, creating nearly four acres of prime real estate at the heart of the campus.

Two new buildings, one at the east end and the other at the west end above the garage, are arranged around a landscaped oval

Burton D. Morgan Hall Denison University, Granville, Ohio
2001–2003

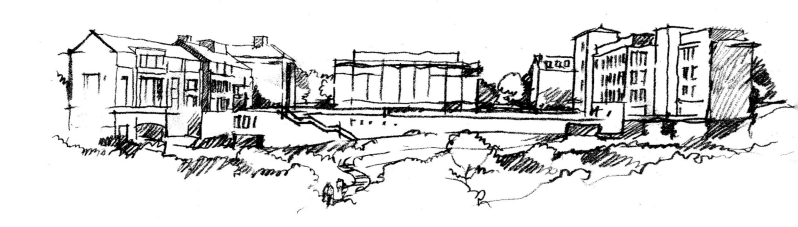

or Campus Common. The siting creates a new forecourt to the existing student center building and a unique outdoor living room for the entire Denison community.

The gateway building, Burton D. Morgan Hall, on the east edge of the Common, provides a new point of entry for campus visitors and houses a variety of academic and administrative functions. Transparency is used as a device to encourage movement through and engagement with the larger campus sequence. A three-story glass lobby, with views to the chapel and the landscaped green, is a physical manifestation of community and communication among faculty, students and alumni. A bridge that connects to adjacent academic buildings and the pavilion affords direct access to the garage. Both forms are rendered in glass and steel and maximize the sense of transparency between the built elements. A distinct sense of discovery and interaction is celebrated as part of the visitor experience as one moves through the building. Being able to drive under the Burton Morgan building provides a ceremonial gateway to the campus and an added dimension to experiencing its heart. This great room

1

Previous page Brick piers supporting large expanses of glass and an intimate lantern dormer characterize the facade facing the Common.

1 A series of small areas within the larger oval offer places for respite in the sequence through campus.
2 Aerial view of the Campus Common shows its placement among the academic heart of campus.

Next page **1** A primary campus road travels under the Burton D. Morgan building. The 380-car parking garage, located under the landscaped oval, has effectively removed cars from the center of campus.
2 Ground level plan of the entire Campus Common initiative, including the **a** Burton D. Morgan building, **b** Slayter Union and **c** Talbot Hall.

2

1

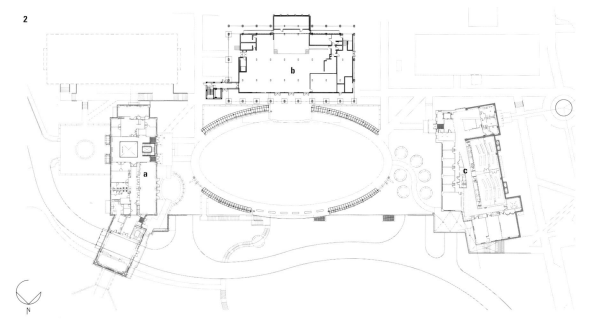

2

was projected out into the landscape, capturing magnificent views on the three major facades.

The landscaped Campus Common acts as a key pedestrian linkage between the academic and residential parts of campus. The previous arrangement of buildings acted as a terminus to the pedestrian and vehicular traffic through the campus, abruptly interrupting the

1

north/south flow. With a compelling new two-acre open space as an organizing device and a gateway building that encourages interaction, pedestrians are now drawn through to the edge of campus. At the same time, vehicular traffic is directed below this precinct into an underground garage. The new separation of paths for pedestrians and vehicles, together with a significant open space, restores the visual clarity and pastoral tradition of the university. The $60 million project was completed in just three years. ■

Previous page The building acts as the organizing device for a new arrival sequence through campus.

1 With a generous use of glass and metal, the circulation core creates many opportunities for interaction and discussion.
2 Entry level plan
3 Lounge areas animate both the lower level and Common level.

Next page A lantern-like roof form draws light vertically through the public circulation.

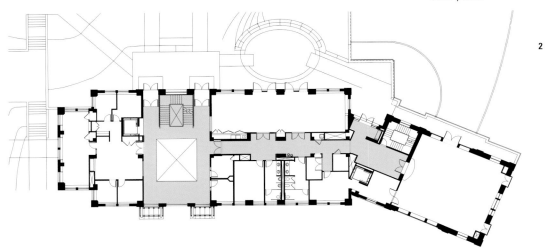

2

3

Over the course of less than a decade, the teaching and delivery of the life sciences at Denison University was completely reimagined. The transformation of the university's Sputnik-era science facilities began with a review of the way the academic curriculum was delivered and the changing pedagogical approach to science education. The physical expression of the new Talbot Hall of Biological Science reflects an interdisciplinary, student-centered and research-centered approach to learning.

Circulation is organized to take advantage of the interaction between departments, with primary laboratories and offices along a double-loaded corridor. Ample display walls and a curved island containing support functions within the generously sized corridor allow for discussion, activity and information to happen outside the labs and offices and into the life of the building. Smaller independent research laboratories and vertical circulation anchor the ends of a modified barbell scheme. Informal study and lounge spaces are created in the infill between zones of activity.

The facade facing the Common features a more traditional rhythm of brick and glass, while the facade oriented toward the residential and academic precincts is composed of longer expanses of crisp curtainwall. This floods the larger laboratories with natural light and allows for a more contemporary vocabulary befitting a science facility. Throughout the design and construc-

Talbot Hall of Biological Science Denison University, Granville, Ohio
2001–2003

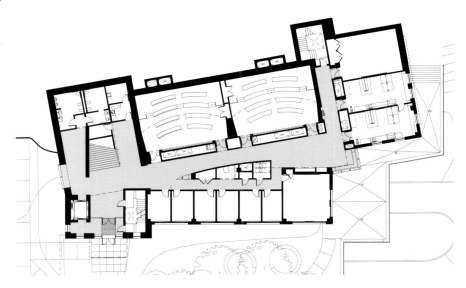

1

2

tion process, sustainable approaches that maximize first cost and operational savings were explored. The roofing material is a white membrane to reflect heat and reduce cooling costs. Offices have operable windows. The mechanical system almost shuts down over the weekend, saving energy. Erosion is controlled with vegetation. The buildings have bicycle racks and ample areas designated inside for the storage and collection of recyclables. Natural lighting is plentiful, but excess heat and glare are avoided through sun shades, low-E coated glass and fritted glass. The laboratories in

the life science building are kept under negative pressure (air is returned at a faster rate than supplied) so that chemical fumes are removed.

With an expansive new green oval that links the three major buildings on the new science quadrangle, the boundaries immediately became blurred between the inside and outside of buildings, social and study space, administrative and academic uses, and many other functional hierarchies. ■

Previous page Facade facing the Common utilizes a more traditional composition of punched windows with layered brick and precast accents.

1/2 Generous areas for informal discussion and meeting have been carved out of the primary circulation.
3 The life sciences building establishes a new identity for the sciences on campus. Light metal trellises delineate the form of the oval.

Next page A curved island within the lower level corridor separates office areas from the large laboratories.

3

1

1 Corners are flooded with natural light and offer both fixed and moveable furnishings for small group work.
2/3 Facing the academic core of campus, both the organic chemistry laboratory (top) and biology laboratory (bottom) are organized with a large band of glass curtainwall.

Next page The main entry lobby from the campus side features ample areas for small groups to gather.

2

3

Led by a mission of linking curriculum with action, this private independent school's new LEED-certified science facility teaches students the responsibility of personal action. The coeducational boarding high school of approximately 400 students, located in Alexandria, Virginia, began with an invited design competition. The goal was to express the functional requirements of scientific inquiry spaces with imagery that celebrates a new way of learning.

Recognizing that the building could be a teaching tool, the solution supports the idea of creating global citizens by measuring the impact of individuals and the larger campus community and creates a tangible link to hands-on learning. Education for sustainability (ESD) is a multidimensional concept that goes far beyond the physical classroom. In fact, it assumes that the school's buildings and grounds, as well as its local community, are the natural extensions of the classroom.

The program of spaces includes biology, physics and chemistry teaching laboratories, a 50-seat lecture room, a science reference library, eight classroom/laboratory spaces, faculty offices and a glass rotunda.

The main entry sequence is organized by a glass rotunda that encourages visitors to move through the building. It is also the ceremonial heart of the sciences complex. This hinge between the bars of classroom space encourages faculty and student interaction, and also functions as a multipurpose meeting and reception area.

Baker Science Center Episcopal High School, Alexandria, Virginia
2003–2005

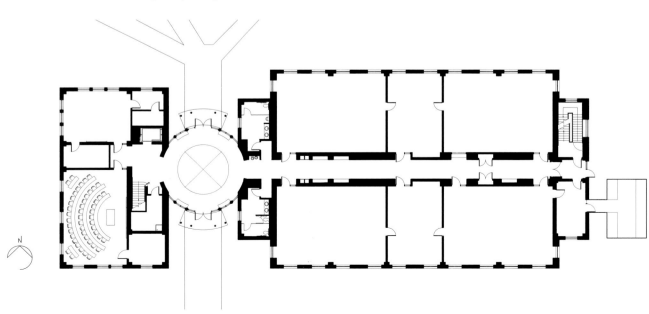

Previous page The steel-framed rotunda is a central meeting place.

1 Interior features include porcelain tile flooring, walk-off mats at the entry, and linoleum on the second level. Daylight floods 90 percent of interior spaces.
2 Aerial campus view shows how the assemblage of forms work together.

Next page Sustainable exterior approaches include the use of 100 percent recycled plastic for the shingled roof, high performance glazing and regionally manufactured brick.

1

2

Water management is a primary energy reduction strategy, including a 14,000-gallon roof rainwater collection system with an underground collection tank. It provides more than 200,000 gallons/year for reuse. A 75 percent reduction of potable water is also possible through the reuse of graywater systems. ▪

Designed within strict Historic District Commission guidelines on the island of Nantucket, this collection of gray-shingled buildings sits on a private site overlooking the Atlantic Ocean to the north and conservation land to the east and south. The family wished to use the house as a vacation retreat year-round and accommodate visitors and family members while retaining a sense of privacy and enclosure.

The complex is composed of three main buildings—the main house, the guest house and the garage—organized by two courtyards. Arriving in the main entry court, visitors glimpse the ocean beyond, but the full view of the sea is revealed as guests move into the private quarters of the interior courtyard. A lighthouse-like tower marks the main entrance and beckons visitors within.

The main house is composed of four volumes and organized by an exterior walkway that links the forms. Each element appears as if the additions occurred over time and works together to provide a soothing rhythm of open space and buildings. By breaking down these elements and connecting them with smaller passages, windows and large expanses of glass are maximized. A variety of window sizes adds to the facade composition, echoing the tradition of farm homesteads.

Interior walls and ceilings are a combination of poplar tongue-and-groove board and batten, with horizontal reveals and matched boards. Interior surfaces are painted in a soft, consistent high-gloss palette to reflect light and create shadow depth throughout the day. The

Summer Residence Nantucket, Massachusetts
1992–1996

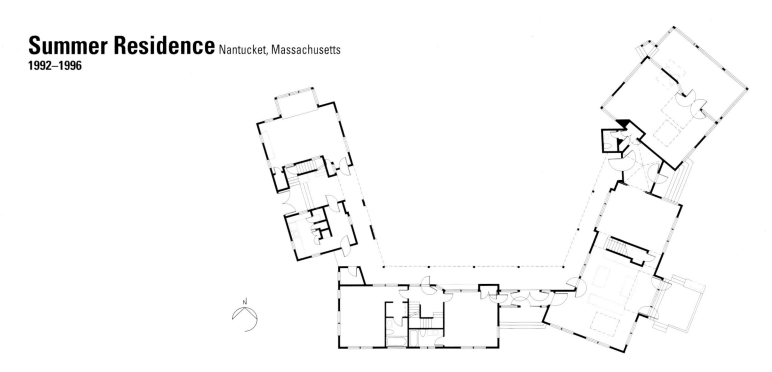

interior is also unified by an abundance of natural wood materials. Dramatic scissor trusses, clear maple floors and brick fireplaces form a natural complement to the painted surfaces and add to the visual interest of interior surfaces.

Previous page A variety of window styles recalls the vernacular of New England farm buildings.

1 Stair detail
2 A game room on the second level overlooks the main gathering areas.

Overleaf The assemblage of small-scale volumes breaks down the scale of the entire house and creates separation between the main house and guest quarters.

Furnishings for the house are scaled for comfort and family use. The tones of sea, sky and sand work with the subdued and sun-bleached landscape. ■

Set in a densely settled Cambridge neighborhood, this unusual wooded property was the site of a street that had been planned but never cut. A previous developer proposed a line of 22 row houses, but the concept was never realized.

The solution sites a single-family residence as part of a larger landscape plan that respects the natural flow and organization of the land with waves of single plant drifts and grass heights. By siting the house deeper into the heart of the site, its connection to the street is preserved, while creating sweeping, private vistas of the bucolic site. Visitors approach the house by a long, narrow drive and experience the sequence of the site from the public realm of the street to the private interior realms of the family. The courtyard is the organizing device for several distinct volumes of space: a kitchen/eating pavilion, a living pavilion and a sleeping pavilion.

The traditional neighborhood includes many clapboard-sided houses with Victorian and other wood details. In deference to this context, the volumes are clad in ship-lapped redwood clapboard of varying lengths. Each volume features slightly different details and widths of siding, which contribute to breaking down the scale and accessibility of the forms. Exterior details include standing-seam zinc roofs and zinc downspouts, with warm granite paving in the courtyards and patios. Granite chimneys and zinc-coated

Five Lowell Street Residence Cambridge, Massachusetts
1999–2001

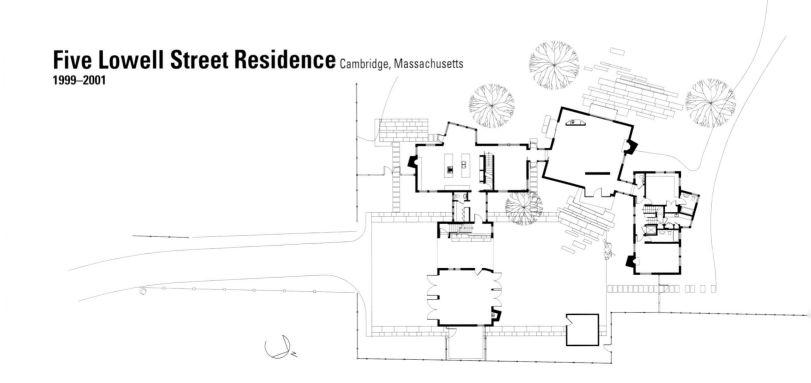

Previous page The glass artist Thomas Patti created a custom installation for the front door bay that changes throughout the day from transparent to opaque.

1 The lower height connectors between forms are clad in zinc.
2 Detail of the glass and steel front door
3 Granite chimneys and paving contrast with the wood siding and zinc downspouts.
4 The kitchen bay sits at an angle to the rectilinear building volume.
5 Interior of the informal dining area

1   **2**

3

4

5

downspouts are the vertical elements that punctuate the horizontal banding of the siding.

The first volume includes an apartment over a storage area. Cars move into the sheltered interior courtyard. At the right, the two volumes of eating/living are each articulated with complementary but distinct materials. The expansive glass front door bay contrasts with the wood siding and smaller punched openings on the second level. The glass installation at the front

entry creates a shimmering curtain that both protects and welcomes.

The three pavilions are connected by narrow, single-height halls clad in a zinc skin, with composed large glass openings. On the interior of the court-yard, smaller punched openings on the second level respond to the private nature of the spaces. The rear/south elevation features larger and more frequent openings that look out onto a private, grassy expanse. The kitchen/eating pavilion and private living pavilion are orthogonal forms with asymmetrically placed roofs that create separation between the forms and capture private views of the landscape. Each of the flanking volumes also contain bays set at slight angles to create a collage of forms that delineates movement around the buildings. More public functions of kitchen, dining and living areas are laid out along a spline of circulation that offers views between rooms and creates natural connections between the spaces. An understated use of color and detail are a soothing backdrop to a dynamic art collection that is placed both inside and out. ◼

Overleaf A glass monitor and over-scaled glass doors suffuse the living area with natural light. The double-height living room allows for the display of large-scale artworks.

1 Sitting area and small office space are open to the kitchen work and reading areas.
2 A limestone fireplace in the living room

1

2

Located just outside the growing city of Orlando, Florida, this new office complex is organized by a 2.2-mile palm-lined boulevard, creating another front door to Disney's Celebration community. Along this major boulevard, a series of interventions knits together a sequence of arrival. As a key marker along Celebration Boulevard, these office buildings echo a variety of styles. This series of individual buildings, created in the Celebration Modern style, reflects art moderne and art deco influences, characterized by sleek lines and sparse but effective ornamentation. A double row of Washington palms lines the entire boulevard, highlighting an expanse of linear parkland for employees. The buildings are organized to include sitting areas under the shade of trees and trellises along their frontage. The trellises also create attractive entrances to pedestrian-friendly parking rooms adjacent to all buildings. ■

Next page The complex is scaled to create a distinct identity from the street, as well as a series of outdoor pedestrian rooms between buildings.

Celebration Office Building Celebration, Florida
2001–2002

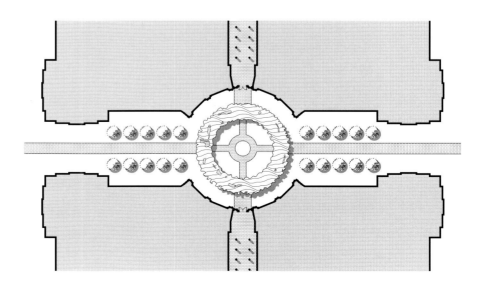

1 Moments in the landscape respond to the ensemble of building forms.

1 Outdoor rooms, shaded by trellises, link the passages between buildings.

Celebration, Florida is synonymous with strong planning principles that create and support community. By combining architecture, education, health and technology in new ways, the town has experienced rapid growth over the past decade. Celebration is home to more than 9000 residents, with a thriving town center and a series of contiguous, integrated neighborhoods. Thirty-six acres have been designed to contain a series of neighborhoods that support interactive learning and provide innovative technology linkages for communication throughout the community. Mirroring the pace of development in the housing sector and the pressure for additional space on a fast-track basis, the School District began to look at alternative delivery methods for its burgeoning student population. In a unique collaboration, the design team partnered with the local School District and a private developer to deliver a new high school for 2000 students.

Constraints of budget and time were viewed as an opportunity to think differently about the choice of materials in this South Florida setting. Using tilt-up construction for concrete forms, inlaid with simple patterns, allowed for construction of all exterior walls over the course of just a few months. The exterior facades feature a simple composition of materials and a complementary palette of colors that change in varying light conditions. The entire 300,000-square-foot complex was constructed in just 20 months.

Site organization is based on the town planning tenets established within Celebration. A wide public boulevard links the shared

Celebration High School Celebration, Florida
2000–2002

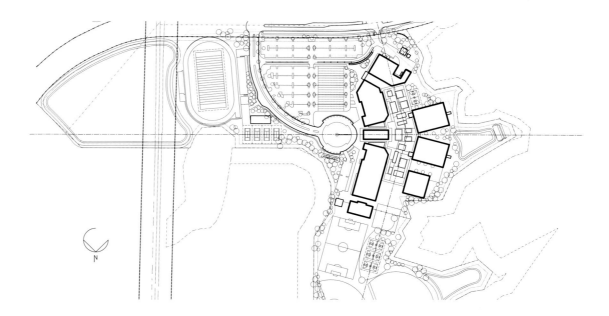

Previous page Screened stair
towers and curving roof forms are
the primary locus for entry.

1 Drop-off shows the splaying of
the plan.
2 In the strong Florida sunshine,
patterns in the concrete forms
create interest and shadow
throughout the day.
3 Ground level plan

1

2

public programs (dining,
library, gymnasium and
auditorium) across the
site. Seen from the main
thoroughfare, the school's
public face is punctuated
by a series of storefront
pavilions with perfo-
rated metal and louvered
entrance details. A center
courtyard with raised bed

planters anchors a series
of adaptable classroom
arrangements. The school
includes flexible, collaborative learning classrooms
that can be arranged by a
team of teachers according
to curricular and student
needs. Flexible technology
and interior wet areas for
science, art and other proj-

3

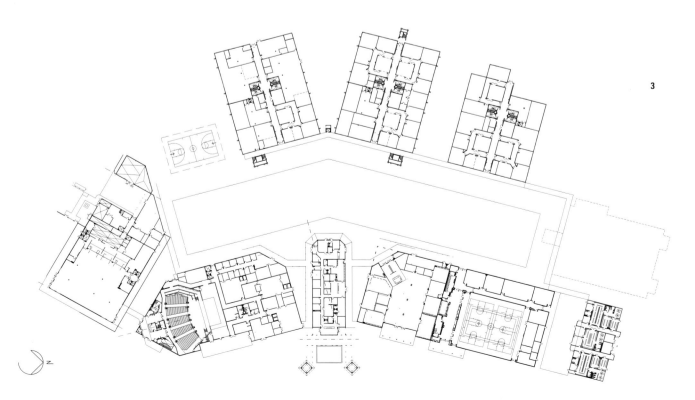

ects respond to new learning groups and styles with minimal disruption. The exterior forms are linked by a procession of shaded arcades that protects against the strong Florida sun and articulates differing scales. Entries, arcades and courtyards link the students with the outdoors throughout the temperate seasons. The combination of precast and concrete panels are played against perforated metal awnings and screens in a palette of warm colors. ■

4 A shaded arcade provides protection from the harsh sun.
5 Roof trellises also provide shade. The classroom wings are organized around the exterior courtyard.

1 A distinctive canopy roof floats above the main entry, providing a recognizable marker from the adjacent boulevard.

Overleaf Detail of the metal trellis system

From its humble beginnings in 1930 as the Garden Center of Greater Cleveland, the mission of the Cleveland Botanical Garden has remained constant: to nurture, inspire and protect the natural world. In the early 1960s, the garden found a permanent home on the site of the former Cleveland Zoo, a pivotal location in the city's cultural nexus. While the center explored the natural evolution of balancing people, plants and the environment, a bold plan for a reimagined visitor center within the heart of established gardens began to take shape. Transforming the institution from a small garden center to a vibrant destination experience took the team nearly a decade, with travel across the globe.

An extensive expansion and renovation plan began with the reconfiguration of building systems and amenities of the original 1960s-era Garden Center and the creation of a new front door into the natural world. There are three recognizable elements to the project: a reconfigured administration building, a new visitor center and a distinct immersion glasshouse. Each is articulated in a distinct palette of materials.

The visitor center is characterized by a sweeping curved entry form and acts as a forecourt and organizing device for the beloved gardens and the original orthogonal Garden building. The curved sandstone facade of the addition reorients visitors into the Garden complex, creates a new front door to the community, and forms a processional entrance court along the eastern edge of the site. Central to the design approach is the development of a vibrant educational/exhibit path throughout the visitor experience. Visitors enter the entrance

Cleveland Botanical Garden Cleveland, Ohio
1996–2003

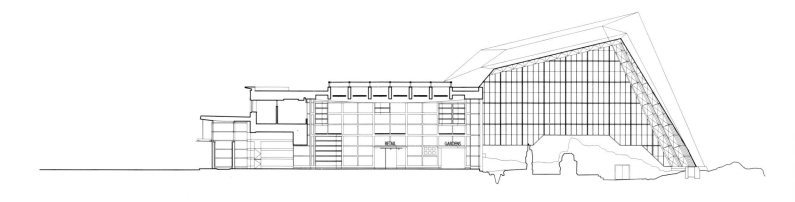

lobby, flooded with natural light and softened with an interior palette of maple and aluminum details. Moving into the interior lobby, or ellipse, visitors can glimpse the exotic plant world through a 28-foot window onto the glasshouse. Two primary circulation paths are delineated: the educational path through the glasshouse and the social path to other amenities, including the gift shop, garden café, multipurpose meeting rooms and gardens beyond.

The third component is an 18,000-square-foot glass conservatory or glasshouse, which is divided into two distinct biomes, together with a working greenhouse. To expand the sense of immersion, the structure of the glasshouse takes its cues from natural geometric forms of quartz crystal, utilizing quadrilateral and triangular planes. Steel tube trusses are set in a regular module and spanned by a light and irregular system of custom aluminum extrusions,

1

2

Entry page Entry lobby view of the forest of columns and section through the lobby.

Previous page 1 Visitors move through the exterior garden rooms to the glasshouse.
2 A cluster of tree-like columns at the front entry

1 Fabrication of the column cluster at the front entry
2 Early concept sketches of the crystalline forms
3 View into the desert-like biome of Madagascar
4 Ground floor plan: **a** ticket office and lobby forecourt; **b** lobby; **c** working greenhouse; **d** Madagascar biome; **e** Costa Rica biome; **f** gift shop; **g** meeting room; **h** circulation to gardens; **i** cafe and entrance out to gardens; **j** outdoor terrace

which allows for traditional lapped glazing. The skin is inspired by early lightweight glasshouse construction techniques of the Victorian era. Individual lapped glass panels are quarter-inch-thick laminated safety glass in two-foot lengths, which allows for maximum light capture. The unusual glasshouse is the only one of its kind that shows how

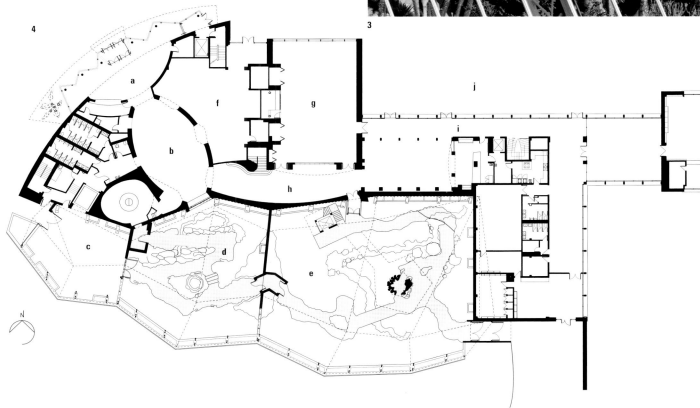

GARDENS

Gardens
Clark Hall
Café
Library
Education Wing

GIFT SHOP

plants, animals, geology and climate interact in delicate balance. Two distinct environments feature more than 350 species of exotic plants and 50 species of butterflies, insects, birds and other animals. Visitors first step into Madagascar, a spiny desert environment that features towering cliffs, massive rock outcroppings and trees that seem to grow upside down. After passing through a transparent airlock, visitors are then transported across the globe to the tropical cloud forest conditions of Costa Rica, where controlled misting systems keep humidity at the proper balance and create a suspended cloud. The educational curriculum is designed for repeat visitors, from the educational needs of the local community to first-time visitors from the world over. The educational immersion experience of the two distinct biomes is carefully balanced with strict technical imperatives of maintaining and preserving rare plant and animal collections. ▪

Previous page The elliptical lobby acts as a central organizing device for circulation.

1 The growing forest can be seen as plants have acclimated in the Costa Rica biome.
2 Section through the lobby

Next page Quarter-inch laminated safety glass is shingled in a traditional glasshouse construction.

1

2

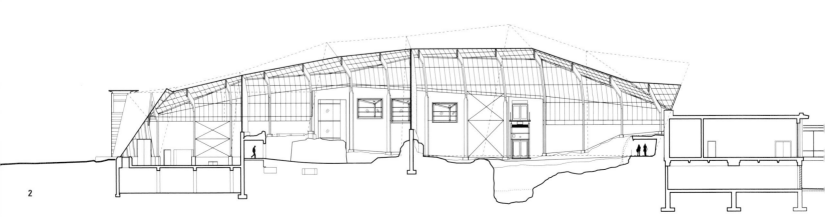

1

2

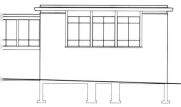

Overleaf As the misting begins, visitors are transported into the cloud forest.

1 At night, the envelope becomes highly transparent and offers a glimpse of the exotic natural world within the biomes.
2 Section through the glasshouse

An existing octagonal-shaped building from the 1960s was the primary identity for the graduate programs in law at this prestigious midwestern university. The challenge was to expand the facilities and update existing conditions commensurate with the Law School's fine reputation.

This 40,000-square-foot building (part new construction and part renovation) with its symmetrical row of soaring brick piers reinforces the strong civic character of the Law School. Massing and materials, while matching those of the existing building, have been reinterpreted into an open pavilion composed of brick columns, monumental glass windows and a dramatic steel truss roof system.

The new construction houses classrooms, student offices and a lounge. The lounge space is open to an exposed structural truss that spans the length of the addition. Two open stairwells connect the two levels of the addition.

A new moot courtroom seats 90 students, a jury and up to three judges. This classroom-courtroom of the future allows for videoconferencing and inter-campus video seminars. The floor system has been designed with a completely integrated electronics network grid that allows access to power, telephone and fiber-optic networks for any future furnishings layout.

The phased project also includes renovation of the law library, faculty offices and a new computer cen-

Law School Library Addition Case Western Reserve University, Cleveland, Ohio
1995–1997

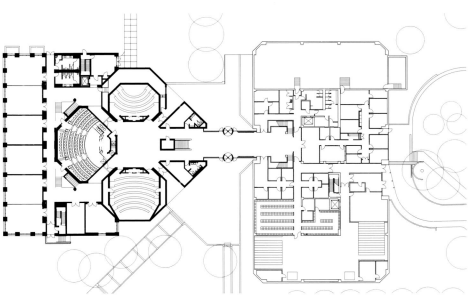

Previous page A grand stair is the new gathering place for the Law School complex.

1 Skylights separate old and new areas and bring light into the center of the circulation.
2 The renovated moot court
3 The library features a transparent wall that allows a visual connection between rooms.

ter. To maximize connections between spaces and optimize light capture, a series of transparent walls is used within the library volume. Circulation and reference areas of the library also improve accessibility and integrate new technology. ■

The International Retail and Manufacturers' Showcase is the $95 million center for Disneyland Paris' commercial district, providing a much-needed regional retail facility. The development serves as a catalyst for the surrounding area's planned urban growth and sets the architectural vocabulary for a sweeping area of the city.

The challenge was to create a retail destination, housing unique retailers and manufacturers from around the world, in a language that evokes a vibrant street environment. The industrial site had few landmarks or context precedents. By taking cues from historic European market precedents such as Les Halles and local paysages, the scale of the entire complex is animated at the street level.

The project is comprised of two basic components. The first element is a 969,000-square-foot traditional French and European shopping center, which features a 280,000-square-foot Hypermarket as the major anchor, as well as other shops and restaurants. The second component is 160,000-square-foot Manufacturers' Showcase, featuring manufacturers, fashion labels and specialty shops from around the world.

The traditional shopping is housed in an experiential shopping mall that spans a busy railway link and serves as an anchor for the expansive development. The showcase is configured as a more traditional French village street, with shop access from the exterior. Parking is part structured and part

EuroDisney's International Retail and Manufacturers' Showcase Paris, France
1995-2001

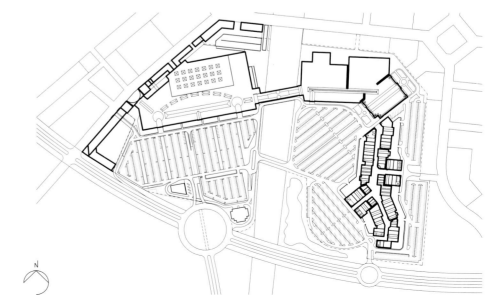

Previous page The glass roof of the Hypermarket recalls European market traditions.

1 People are the primary animators of the space.
2 Aerial view of the main entrance to the village.
3 The market elevation utilizes a consistent rhythm of small and large bays.
4 Ground level view of the market.

surface, accommodating more than 5000 cars.

The primary challenge was to create a unique, imaginative retail environment that breaks the mold of traditional shopping center facilities. While respecting the fundamentals of retail planning, this new expression immerses visitors and transports them to a wholly planned town center. The model is premised on the integration and articulation of distinct elements of a town center, with mixed-use shopping, educational spaces, office and commercial uses. Its cost-effective real estate principles and contextual response to traditional French influences has been tremendously successful for the owner.

The design and development of a new town center seamlessly integrates indoor and outdoor components. The buildings were created to promote the movement and comfort of pedestrians who live, work, shop and/or visit the city. ◼

1

2

4

1 Aerial view of the outlet village
shopping area

The distinctive shape of this modern housing tower in Orlando, Florida is in response to the L-shaped site and desire to maximize the number of units with lake and city views. The site is part of a larger 85-acre tract, with a nine-acre lake as the primary organizing device.

The program includes 233 residential apartments, associated support spaces and a 450-car parking garage. The 24-story tower also houses a single-unit penthouse and three duplex units. On the lower levels, a multilevel parking structure with a street-level courtyard separates vehicular and pedestrian access. Other street-level amenities include a health club, pool terrace, and private gardens for a number of units. Each element of the project, from tower to parking garage, has

been designed to respond to a complicated context of large- and small-scale buildings surrounding this significant lakeside Orlando site.

Layers of color and material work both horizontally and vertically in the massing. An orange and yellow tower with an illuminated crown is a locus for community on the downtown skyline. An attached 14-story horizontal "wave" building recalls Lake Eola and adds a cool transparency to the tower's Florida palette. Narrow bands of pigmented stucco support large expanses of glass to produce a lighter skin. The penthouse towers, crowned with a metal brise-soleil, are distinctly lighter in tone. The punched super grid of the tower and the horizontal waves and blue banding of the lower section, combined with the

The Waverly at Lake Eola Orlando, Florida
1997–2001

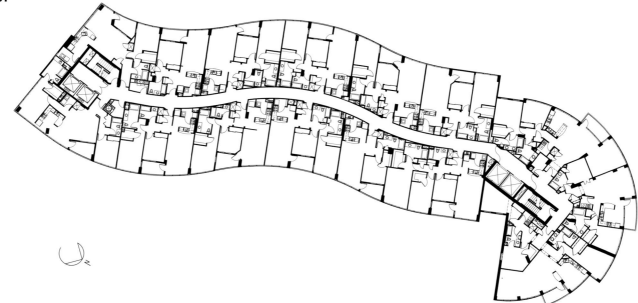

building's overall abstract forms, create a contemporary address in a town known for its significant resort architecture.

Public areas in the interior continue this loose expression, with complementary colors, forms and furnishings. ■

Previous page At night, the building is a new landmark on the skyline.

1/2 The entrance lobby utilizes similar curves and colors of the Florida coast.

Next page The unique floor plans offer dramatic views and vistas.

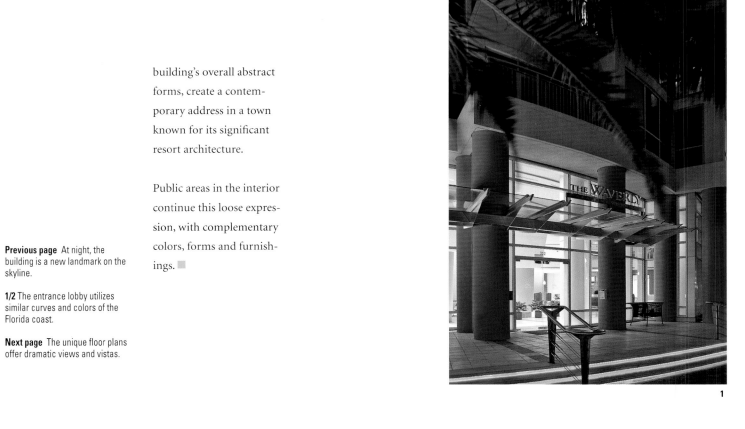

1

2

This vital crossroads site is located just three blocks north of the U.S. Capitol. The unusual triangular shape of the site is derived from Pierre L'Enfant's original conception of the city. L'Enfant's Master Plan envisioned a series of radiating grand boulevards that sliced through the city grid, creating a limited number of special triangular sites. These sites were natural focal points that became centerpieces of neighborhoods and distinct locations for monuments, parks and community gathering.

As a key conduit to the civic center of the city, the street plane is a critically important barometer of urban life. The site, which had been abandoned for many years, included a designated National Park Service green space that had fallen into disrepair and misuse. Many years of industrial contamination and pollution as a result of its previous use as a gas station also created a brownfield. Numerous developers had looked at the site for potential reuse, but found the narrow shape of the parcel and strict zoning requirements as a great hindrance to a viable commercial floor plate.

The neighborhood is filled with the familiar masonry and bowfront bays of Washington, soldiers standing in line in deference to the U.S. Capitol. Along the streetwall on both the eastern and western edges, the typical Washington masonry infill allowed little respite for the pedestrian experience. Previous proposals sug-

National Association of Realtors Washington, D.C.
2001–2004

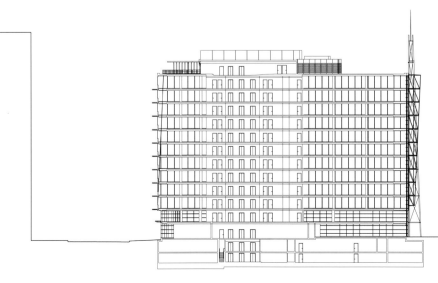

gested a similar solid masonry wall, with small bays that projected out four feet from the facade, as allowed by zoning. The successful solution proposed a modern interpretation of the zoning regulation for bay windows. By treating the entire facade as a projecting bay, the building form became a single sweeping bowfront along the street edge. This created a much more viable floor plate for commercial development. Exterior materials were chosen to be a light and reflective counterpoint to the heavy masonry neighbors. With the building filling almost the entire site plan, it was also important to reclaim the immediacy of the street as an integrated part of the building solution. Welcoming plazas, restoration of the NPS park, and a careful reknitting of the street fabric into the north-south sequence of the city flow is central to the design solution.

The building tapers from 60 feet wide on the south to about 10 feet on the north. These dimensions accentuate the building's 130-foot height. The high-density building is a celebration of a Washington crossroads with spectacular views of the Capitol from the upper floors and roof deck and dynamic east-west views slicing across the north-

south street. Sheathed in curved planes of a high-performance coated glass, the building skin reflects changing conditions of sun and clouds, summer and winter. Depending on the season and time of day, the two facades appear to slip past each other in hues ranging from deep blue to aquamarine and seagreen. A double-glazed curtain-wall utilizes a new type of glazing, Viracon Radiant Low-E (VRE) Insulating Glass, which contains a coating that minimizes the transfer of heat through radiation and provides an improved shading coefficient. Architectural

Previous page The flytower at the northern tip of the building acts as both symbolic marker and hinge between facade planes.

1 A soothing water feature punctuates the hardscape plaza.
2 Outdoor seating animates the street plane.
3 The triangular site had historically been a key marker, designated for an important building or monument.

Next page In the spirit of Washington's strong east-west axial avenues, visitors move past the bowed facades in a sweeping gesture toward the Capitol.

shading is provided by a brise-soleil on the south elevation.

Other sustainable features include use of more than 50 percent of materials with recycled contents; a 30 percent improvement over ASHRAE 90.1-1999 high efficiency performance standards; a 30 percent reduction in the use of potable water; and a rainfall collection system on the low albedo roof, which is directed to an 8500-gallon cistern in the garage of the building. Current and future tenants are strongly linked to the larger environmental impact of building, community and energy consumption. The primary owner/occupant is housed on four floors, with the remaining floors available for tenant leasing. The design team worked

1

2

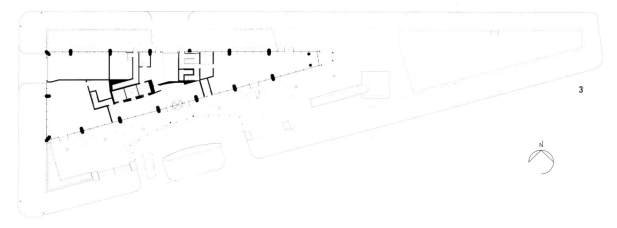

3

1 Roof deck meeting areas
2 Typical office plan
3 Ground floor plan
4 Main reception areas and core feature a fast-growing eucalyptus veneer paneling.

Next page The monumental stair between the main client floors encourages circulation and interaction.

4

Previous page Special conference areas at the northern end of the building act as an anchor to the typical office floor.

1 Movement and rest are articulated along the street plane. The former brownfield site is now a safe neighborhood destination and a catalyst for urban renewal.

Overleaf Glass and soft, reflective surfaces are brought into the interior materials, further blurring the boundary between inside and outside, public and private.

with the owner to develop mandatory fit-out guidelines for tenants. The result is a commercial urban office space that is both economically viable and environmentally sustainable. Celebrating this crossroads as a symbol of the workplace of the future is truly in the spirit of L'Enfant's original vision. ■

The William Oxley Thompson Library is the main library of The Ohio State University. The original library was built in 1913, enlarged in 1947–1951 and expanded again in 1977. Its landmark location at the heart of the campus and the western terminus of the historic Oval reinforces the library's position as a symbolic and intellectual crossroads.

Since its opening nearly a century ago, however, dramatic changes have occurred in campus life, library design, technology applications and service delivery within the library. Ohio State has 20 libraries holding nearly 6 million volumes, with one-third of these holdings housed in the Thompson Library. Adding to this pressure is the reduction of reader seats within the original library and the transformation of the closed stack tower into renovated areas for readers within miles of narrow shelving. The competition between patron services and the growing need for additional space for the collection has continued to intensify, even with the recent construction of an off-site book depository.

After a thorough review of feasibility options, the recommended plan reinforces the axial relationship of the main library with the Oval by reconnecting the new west addition with the main library circulation, and expanding the presence of the library to the growing western end of campus. In addition, a key component of the project is the restoration of the original library's main reading rooms, remodeling of the interior atrium,

Thompson Library Addition and Renovation The Ohio State University, Columbus, Ohio
2003–2008

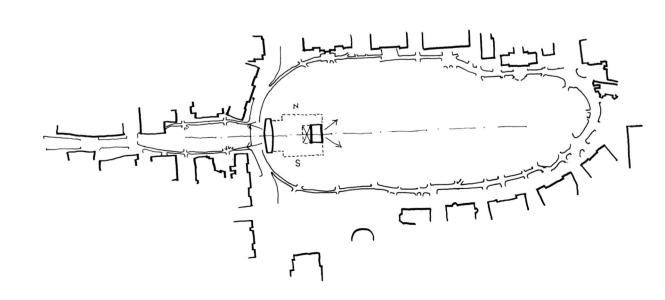

1

Previous page Recognizing the growth at the western edge of campus, the renovated complex's focal point will be a two-story, glass reading room standing two stories above ground.

1 1926 library view
2 The book tower creates a new vista across campus.
3 Readers are welcomed back into the heart of the library experience.

and major improvements and renovations to the stack tower. Given the size and complexity of the program, the project presents a unique opportunity to create an outstanding research library that will serve as a model for the 21st century.

A melding of historic, mid-century and future structures is at the heart of this redefinition of the modern research library. Three key design de-

terminants needed to be resolved: integration of a venerable, historic structure at the center of the campus' main oval; rethinking/replanning of an obsolete 1960s-era stack tower; and definition of a new intervention, embracing IT as central to the learning process.

The solution acknowledges the Oval as the primary organizing mechanism for the overall campus order, with the expanded library

3

2

1 From within, the books are lit, elevating their stature outside the formerly cavernous, dark, closed stack tower.
2 Section across the Oval

at its apex. The existing book tower has been re-imagined as a new interior heart of discovery. The east-west orientation of the tower is at the fulcrum of the library organization, with an atrium and reading rooms on each side of double-height entries. Trays of reader spaces flank the atria on the north-south axis, balancing the internal circulation and bringing the physical presence of books and virtual IT connections together on all major levels of the interior.

The facade composition knits the historic sandstone and traditional details of the original library with a more porous expression for renovation and new construction. Large expanses of glazing and spare details reopen the doors of the library to the entire campus. ■

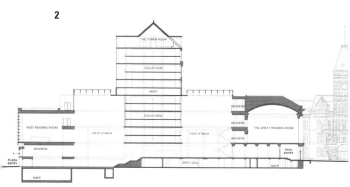

The original Master Plan for Brandeis University was developed by Eero Saarinen and featured individual buildings atop the hilly, pastoral setting as temples, rejecting the traditional closed collegiate quadrangle model. The pavilion-like original Art Museum, built in 1961, is a classic International Style structure. The first phase of the program called for expansion of the 15,000-square-foot museum in an addition of 8800 square feet.

The design concept reinforces the location and identification of the original museum as a temple and graciously defers to it with the siting of the addition. The addition is reached through the grand entrance of the old building, and takes a secondary position behind it. Its location engages and transforms the existing building through a replanned circulation. The arrival sequence begins at the front door of the original museum. Visitors may cross the original gallery to a glass doorway that opens onto a balcony overlooking the new main gallery below. Descending the grand, glass-enclosed staircase between the original building and new wing, with views of nature beyond, visitors enter on the ground level. The play of light and dark, volume and void, is glimpsed throughout the circulation sequence. Walls and surfaces are reduced to fundamental elements and planes. The ceiling is a luminous plane that modulates artificial and natural light and delivers

Lois Foster Wing at the Rose Art Museum Waltham, Massachusetts
1999–2001

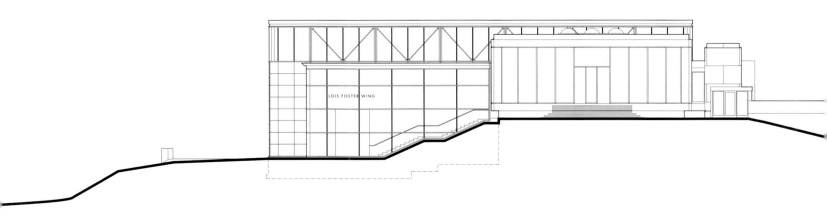

1

2

climate-controlled fresh
air. Exterior materials were
selected to harmonize with
the limestone cladding of
the existing museum, with
simple and elegant materials and details. The reflective skin is a rear-venti-
lated exterior wall system
comprised of sleek and
lightweight ceramic panels
articulated with alumi-
num trim. The legibility
of activities and flexibility
of installations are sup-
ported by an acid-etched
glass clerestory, lined with
adjustable louvers that
control the daylight within

228

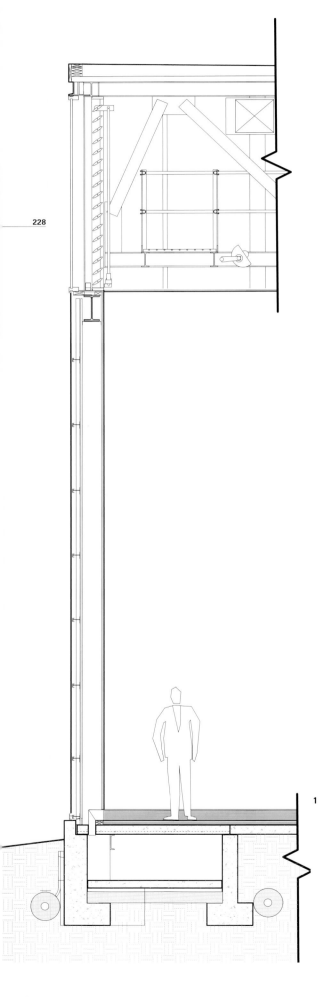

1

2

3

4

Previous page At night, the facade acts as a billboard for the arts and can been seen from deep within the campus core. The stair hall acts as an additional exhibition space.

1 Wall section showing operation of the clerestory.
2 Mechanized louvers control the amount of daylight within the gallery.
3 The clerestory level contains an accessible catwalk above the gallery floor.
4 With thin mullions, the acid-etched glass appears to float.

Next page The 24-foot, two-story galleries can be adapted for any scale and particular requirements for contemporary art.

the gallery space below from complete darkness to full natural light. The combination of diffusion glass and daylight louvers in the clerestory and a luminous ceiling above the gallery creates a warm surface of lighting throughout the gallery for the widest range of installations from full daylight to full darkness. At night, the addition glows, illuminating and representing its changing contents and reinforcing the importance of the arts on campus. ◼

A new communal meeting place is emerging on college campuses, where the athletic, recreational, academic, and social lives of students intersect. This traditional collegiate Gothic college campus in the Midwest is at the forefront of developing a new paradigm for student life by combining a traditional athletic program with these myriad aspects of the collegiate experience. The program includes a 50-meter swimming pool, tennis courts, squash courts, arena basketball courts, theater and film library, multipurpose rooms, study lounges, weight room, a fieldhouse/running track, training rooms, various offices and a small café.

With such an ambitious collection of spaces, the challenge was to find an appropriate vocabulary and scale for a new 250,000-square-foot athletic center. The older parts of the campus were laid out along an organizing spine known as Middle Path. Each new building that was added to this ensemble responded to and shaped the dialogue among its neighbors. As the density along the ridge increased with Kenyon's development, the natural contours of the campus dictated the location of open playing fields below the ridge in an undulating flood plain. The articulated, prominent ridge of buildings, grandly scaled and finely detailed, is the primary image of the college.

The site is located below the primary ridge of the historic campus in a flat and grassy flood plain.

Kenyon Athletic Center Kenyon College, Gambier, Ohio
2001–2005

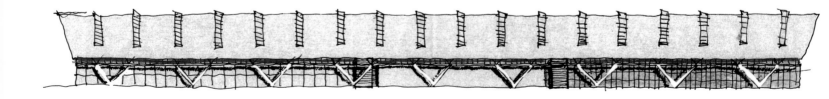

Previous page The interplay of interior materials blends solid and void, transparent and opaque.

1 Primary circulation is organized by a monumental stair that slices through all three levels. Similar to a town square, the stairs and a luminous elevator core work together to create a landmark for circulation.
2 Ground floor plan
3 Basketball arena
4 The fieldhouse can be subdivided for all kinds of indoor activities.

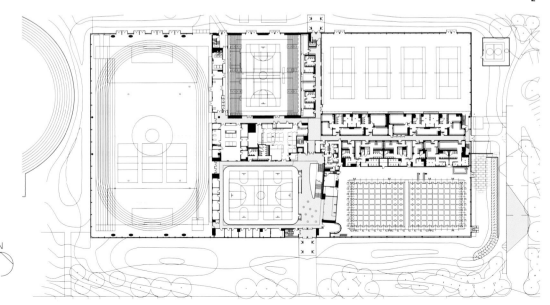

This evocative landscape became the primary motivation for the building's massing, form and scale. The old stone buildings of the campus, located on a hill above the site, have small windows in stone facades that relate well to the human scale. Responding to the rural land of the riverbed below, this new intervention has a simpler form. Its shed-like volume is expressed as a smooth exterior of glass and metal over an exposed steel structure. The sides of the building dip toward the ground, lowering the scale of the building, and following the arc of a ball in play.

The elevations are purposely streamlined with minimal materials to engage the monumental roof form. The three main facades work together to respond to the surrounding athletic fields and neighboring houses in a visually unbroken line. The southern facade wall is composed of internally baffled insulating low-E glass, while a solid wall at the eastern

3

4

Previous page The multipurpose activity court is used throughout the day for recreation, intramural and gathering activities. Perimeter offices and dance studios overlook this primary locus of activity.

1 Detail of southern facade
2 Movement within the stair connects and engages activity on all three levels.

1

elevation is composed of corrugated metal panels. Portions of the western facade elevation are composed of perforated corrugated stainless steel to complete the transition between solid and void.

The structural clarity and hierarchy of the solution alludes to the collegiate Gothic characteristics of the campus, particularly in the expression of vertical tension in the facade. A single roof structure features repetition and structural efficiency. Structural supports are purposely placed so far apart that the roof itself seems to float. The line of glass between the roof and wall becomes a horizon line, and the courts, track and other playing surfaces become the ground plane. The roof profile and noise attenuation are streamlined by locating mechanical systems and their distribution underground.

Visitors enter in the center of the building and disperse out to different venues from a transparent core. Like a town square, the center is an orienting

device and the luminous elevator core and light sculpture are a focal point. Wherever one travels within the building, open vistas across the interior landscape allow participation in many different activities. A monumental stair leads from the front door to public viewing areas for the venues on the second level.

Transparency is used as both a tool and a metaphor. Layers of transparent and opaque materials define precincts of space, which progress from the main stair and create open vistas across the interior

1 As seen in the detail of the roof line and skylights, materials are expressed in layers of transparent and opaque.
2 The boundary between inside rooms and outside spaces is intentionally porous.
3 Upper level plan

Next page Light in the interior of the pool is controlled by several devices, including internally baffled low-E glass.

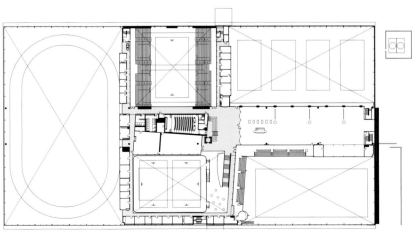

Previous page The fitness area and weight training room act as a common meeting area and community living room for the campus.

1 The 50-meter pool provides space for competitive and recreational swimming.

1 Natural light and warm surfaces create a continuous circulation flow through all three main levels.
2 A custom-designed, programmable light sculpture animates both the ground floor and mezzanine levels.

Next page Light is controlled through the ceramic fritted skylights and creates a warm ambience both day and night.

Overleaf Transparency is intentionally exploited through the use of primary materials, including the vaulted skylight roof and glass envelope.

core. It was important to create a place where everyone could come together on campus, not only for individual fitness and recreation, but also in teams, in groups, and as an entire community. Making connections between different ways of experience is at the core of an active liberal arts education. ■

1

2

Projects in development

1 View along Boylston Street
2 Headhouse view in front of the
Boston Public Library

Next page The building forms
recede to respect the strong
historic vocabulary along the
streetwall.

Copley Square Subway Station
Boston, Massachusetts
2001–2006

Anchoring a prominent corner of Copley
Square, where historic and modern influences
converge, this series of small interventions
was designed to be read as transparent forms
in a solid landscape. The early subway system
entrances were typically granite, with a special
headhouse fronting the Boston Public Library
detailed with ornate iron grillwork. A series
of new steel and glass pavilions reinterprets
materials and proportions of these historic
structures. Transparency is used as a gesture
to allow the interventions to recede from the
streetscape. These background structures also
help to reinforce the renovated historic iron
gatehouses as the primary vocabulary of the
transportation system.

1

2

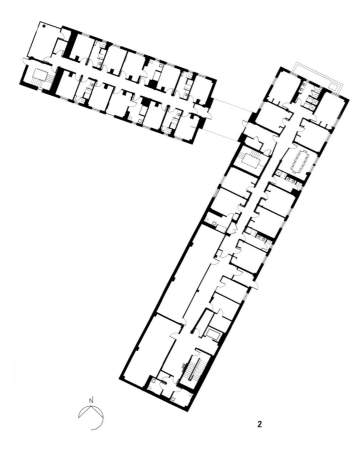

1

1 As seen in the elvation, the building form is stepped in relation to the steep site.
2 Ground floor plan
3 Seen from the primary pedestrian circulation path, the building creates a new sequence through campus.

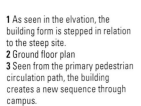

2

Housing Study Tufts University, Medford, Massachusetts
2003–2004

The rise in demand for on-campus student housing, together with the increasing pressure on housing stock in the surrounding community, created a strong need for new residential beds at Tufts University. This study for a new residence hall design includes approximately 150 beds organized in an L-shaped scheme. The main bar building houses freshmen and sophomores; the wing houses juniors, seniors and graduate students. The wing building, containing only singles, also houses visiting faculty and conference attendees. The program includes a three-bedroom faculty penthouse apartment and roof terrace.

As a way of encouraging more social and intellectual interaction among students and faculty, the new residence hall program includes a variety of common spaces for study, meetings and community gatherings. The building design is also a didactic tool, with a link to the Tufts Climate Initiative. Students can see the impact of their actual energy usage on a larger global scale. The design incorporates sustainable design elements in effort not only to achieve LEED accreditation, but also to serve as a more energy efficient model for future buildings at Tufts University. The study led to the successful award of a $500,000 grant from the Massachusetts Renewable Technology Collaborative for the installation of solar panels on the roof. ■

3

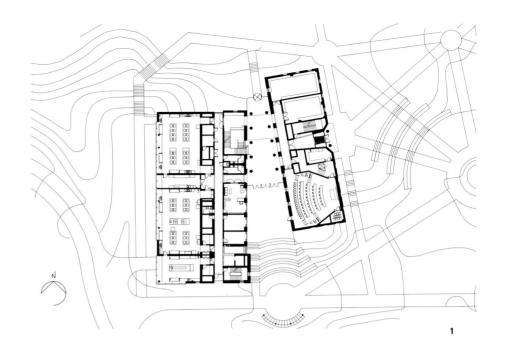

1

Chemistry Building Study Denison University,
Granville, Ohio
2002–2003

Responding to new programmatic partner-
ings, this university-level research building
repurposes an outdated 1960s building with
new construction to double the size of existing
facilities. The existing structure is replanned to
better accommodate new teaching needs, and
reskinned to form a cohesive composition with
the new volume. Two distinct bar forms are
linked by a glass-enclosed entry volume that
establishes a strong connection to the outdoors.
Lounges, social spaces and informal gathering
areas are expressed in large expanses of glass
on the facade. Glass and metal bays wrap the
corners of the facade and fill the main labs with
natural light.

Enclosed courtyard spaces of the atrium spill
out into the landscaped outdoors to the south,
anchoring the new chemistry complex to the
heart of the sciences quadrangle. Nine research
labs, six teaching labs and faculty offices are
located in the existing structure. The new
construction houses large public lecture and
meeting spaces, including classrooms, lecture
halls, seminar rooms, reading room/library
and lounges/student study areas. The program
includes labs for physical and analytical chemistry, general chemistry, organic chemistry,
biochemistry, synthetic research and advanced
synthetic chemistry research. ■

1 Ground floor and site plan
2 Campus elevation
3 The two forms meet in a glass entry volume.

2

3

1/2/3 The two bars are connected by a glass hinge that also acts as a draw for pedestrians through a vital campus crossroads. An outdoor sculpture court brings the arts outside.

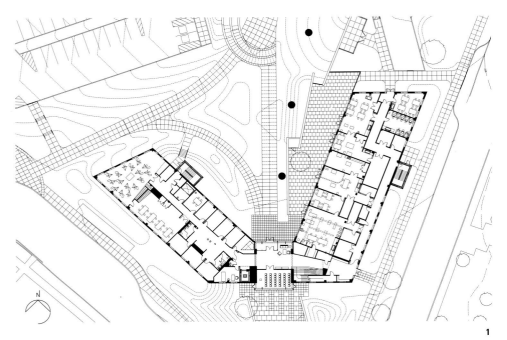

1   2

Visual Arts Center   University of Massachusetts, Amherst, Massachusetts 2004–2008

Located at a key primary entry point on campus, the 51,000-square-foot Visual Arts building for the University of Massachusetts at Amherst creates a dramatic arts gateway on campus, engaging and involving the entire campus community.

The program features a new home for both the dirty and clean studio arts, including print-making, sculpture/clay, photography, painting/drawing, woodworking and metal. The new

building anticipates revolutionary changes brought on by the integration of technology into all of the arts. The program addresses the multidisciplinary trend in art education by creating a central core of resource space and a variety of flexible working studios. Core spaces are available to all students, with the opportunity to create individual expression in flexible studio spaces. To attract a higher caliber of students and faculty, common undergraduate studios and dedicated individual graduate/fac-

ulty studios provide privacy as well as opportunity for community.

The V-shaped plan locates studios and offices along two bar volumes, linked by a glass cube that houses commons functions. Activities supporting campus and community outreach, including a lounge/café space and a variety of gallery and lecture spaces, are located in the most transparent part of the building envelope. ■

1 Site plan
2/3 The academic core is the figurative center to the entire high school campus. Large expanses of glass curtainwall are set against a background composition of brick.

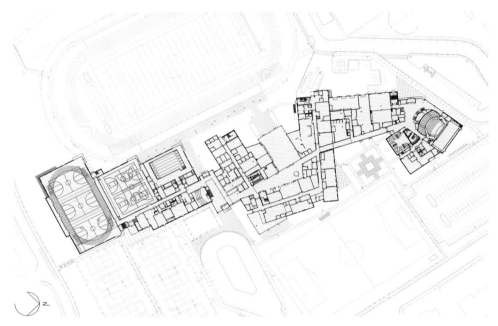

1   2

Newton North High School
Newton, Massachusetts
2005–2009

Site conditions are the primary driver of building form in this new 1950-student high school. Located in a fine-grained residential neighborhood, the building is ordered around a series of courtyards, which are set back from the street to create a sense of enclosure and engagement. During construction, the existing school remains in place and operational on the site. When complete, the original building will be demolished and the athletic fields re-oriented to allow for optimal playing conditions.

Three major volumes containing athletics, the academic core and the theater are linked by a luminous glass lobby that acts as one of two front doors into the school. A separate main entrance is located within the theater volume, allowing for community access after-hours. Programmatically, the new school is predicated on a Main Street plan organization. Taking cues from the existing school, Main Street is enlarged and expanded, traveling both inside and outside in a visually unbroken line.

Within the academic wing, a serpentine-shaped plan with double-loaded corridors brings natural light into every classroom and creates animated vistas across the site. The academic core is the largest volume within the entire assemblage of building forms. Major program areas are articulated with glass and metal accents against a palette of variegated brick. Discrete entry markers are rendered in glass and metal. ■

3

About GUND Partnership

Collaboration by Design
Hilary Lewis

Architecture is never done alone. To design and build a building the architect must form consensus among many actors—patrons, community members, engineers, construction managers—the final product is not the work of a single figure, but rather the result of a well-orchestrated process. The best architects know how to lead participants in the architectural experience to an endpoint that accommodates all. This is never easy, but it is precisely the challenge that architects face daily.

It is unsurprising then that architectural firms tend to mimic internally the process that architects know so well from their relationships with clients. Collaboration is an essential part of the architect's work both within and without the firm. Some architectural organizations achieve this more naturally than others, but most understand the fundamental need for teamwork and the advantage of coordinating the many and distinct talents of the firm's members.

This is clearly the case at Gund Partnership, whose name indicates both the leadership of the firm's founder, Graham Gund, and the organization's attitude towards its people. Gund is a marquee name, well-established since Graham Gund went out on his own in 1971 following his work with Walter Gropius at the former Bauhaus master's own Cambridge-based firm. Clearly, Gund learned his lessons well from the great German modernist. Gropius believed strongly in the coordination of individual efforts—hence the name of *his* firm: The Architects Collaborative.

Gund Partnership is part of that legacy of Gropius, who established in his work at the Bauhaus,

Harvard and eventually at The Architects Collaborative, the very essence of what we consider to be the modern approach to architecture. That is defined by the architect's attempt to provide a solution for a complex problem that comprises site, budget, function and environment. Producing the correct response to a client's request for a new building, master plan or renovation, requires much more than the ability to listen closely to the patron and potential user, it demands a delicate back-and-forth between architect and client. A successful project emerges from a partnership that is formed by the architect, client and community.

Gund Partnership's practice is based on an open collaborative process. Everyone in the firm is encouraged and challenged to promote innovative, intelligent ideas for the design and management of the firm. The four principals, Graham Gund, John Prokos, Youngmin Jahan, and Laura Cabo—all of whom have worked together for over 20 years—share the day-to-day and long-term administrative tasks for the firm. With the respect and trust gained over decades of working with one another, they build consensus rather than engage in a formal hierarchy. While each person may focus on a particular set of design or administrative tasks, decisions are made collectively via active and open discussion.

Principals are project leaders who foster a climate of openness and collaboration for all team members while guiding each project towards its best design solution. The success of this process is evident in the work showcased in this book. While all projects reveal an understanding of light and a deep consideration of context, there is nonetheless a rich variety of design solutions presented here—all the product of a thoughtful and detailed process. Gund Partnership's commitment to collaboration results in the individuality of each project, which evolves out of many factors and the input of multiple architects.

In essence, Gund Partnership is proof of how an organization can expand the reach of a single architect and transform it into a larger vision. This firm consistently creates designs that work well for clients, which are in no way uniform, but are nonetheless recognizably the result of a unified attitude toward architecture. This collection of buildings is the mature oeuvre of a firm that has long been committed to collaboration—with its clients and among its partners. The result is a portfolio of buildings that stand out, yet belong in their communities. That pairing—of individual distinction and coordinated teamwork—precisely describes Gund Partnership itself. ■

Firm Profile

GUND Partnership is an award-winning professional practice committed to the built environment. With more than 100 regional and national awards for design excellence, the firm's projects have in common creative design solutions, spatial interest and well-crafted details.

The core of the practice is centered on a collaborative process to express mission, philosophy and community in a wide variety of planning and design assignments. Founded as Graham Gund Architects in 1971, the firm has evolved and grown into a fully cooperative team with a dedicated leadership group. In 2004, the firm reorganized to become GUND Partnership, acknowledging the long-standing contribution of a core group of collaborators. The current group of principals—Graham Gund, John Prokos, Laura Sanden Cabo and Youngmin Jahan—has practiced together for more than 20 years. In addition, a senior group of architects who have been with the firm for more than a decade comprise the foundation of the project management team.

The staff profile includes a community of approximately 55 individuals. GUND Partnership has long employed sustainable design and green design concepts as part of our approach to siting, program and material expression. Over the past five years, the firm has been at the forefront of developing a seasoned team of designers and planners with an intimate familiarity with LEED design criteria. More than 80 percent of the technical staff are LEED Accredited Professionals.

GUND Partnership is located in Cambridge, Massachusetts in a 70,000-gross-square-foot renovated court complex originally designed by Charles Bulfinch. The building was restored by GUND in 1986 and renovated in 2004.

Architecture is the most public of the arts. As stewards of the public realm, architects must create design solutions that respect the past and also look to the future. Architecture is also process, a fluid interchange of context, function and need. GUND Partnership seeks to balance the competing influences of people, materials and technology in each assignment and create buildings, spaces and environments that elevate people's everyday experiences and sense of community.

As seen in the group of diverse projects included in this monograph, some common threads link the design explorations over the past decade of work. Beginning with a respect for the principles of site and context as form drivers, the projects seek to knit together site, mission and materials in new ways. New and revitalized buildings are often a physical manifestation of the larger ideals and mission of each client. Whether it is an urban or campus intervention or a pristine landscape, the most successful solutions are those that tie into their organizing context. Establishing relationships with the larger context creates a wholeness or fit that also generates a timeless sense of appropriate intervention. At the same time, buildings must acknowledge their surroundings without imitation. This is accomplished through a commitment to human scale, a clear conception of space and its progression and a desire to provide delight through the unexpected.

Many of the projects explore courtyards as an organizing device for building massing. A majority of featured projects are intimately linked to larger campuses and smaller quadrangles, where siting and placement of volumes must work within a greater whole. Several of the residential projects also use the courtyard as a way of breaking down scale, creating a tension between volumes, and linking functions. In urban contexts, where the relationship to the larger street plane is critical to the organization of programmatic functions and building systems, the featured projects are expressly aware of their responsibility as generators of activity at the ground plane.

Material expression has evolved in response to many influences. The level of detail, texture, scale and articulation evolves out of the specifics of the project setting and goals. While some of the earlier work in campus settings has been primarily rendered in masonry, these projects are characterized by their aspiration to be interpretative in nature rather than imitative. This expression has also progressed to a lighter balance of solid and void, with many recent projects exploring transparency and new skin layers as both a tool and a metaphor.

Programmatic influences and layering of functions are linked by a strong shaping of natural light and sequence through spaces. Several trends in educational projects have also shaped projects for other programmatic uses, including the linking of spaces inside and outside and the changing balance of public and private domains. Above all, the projects endeavor to support ways of building community by establishing a comfortable rhythm of built and open space, as well as a hierarchy of pedestrian, vehicular and service needs. To create pleasant environments to live, work and learn, the basic comforts of natu-

Graham Gund FAIA
PRINCIPAL

ral light, materials and air must be provided, but the overall environment must also be comprehensible to its users.

Finally, GUND Partnership believes that the best projects are a collaboration. No project can be successful without the openness, innovation and vision of its client team. We are grateful to a remarkable group of collaborators who have given us the opportunity to explore new ways of seeing, learning and living.

Graham Gund began his career working for Walter Gropius at The Architects Collaborative. He founded the firm that bears his name in 1971. His work has received wide critical acclaim and professional recognition, and has brought the firm more than 100 awards for design excellence. Born in Cleveland, Ohio, Graham was educated at Kenyon College and pursued postgraduate study at the Rhode Island School of Design. He earned a Master of Architecture and a Master of Architecture in Urban Design from the Harvard University Graduate School of Design. In addition, he holds several honorary degrees.

Graham has a legacy of contextually diverse projects noted for their success as both urban fabric and highly usable, engaging public spaces. He has personally overseen more than 3 million square feet of housing projects and more than 100 projects for academic institutions. Mr. Gund is active in New England's cultural arts and architecture communities. He is a trustee of the Museum of Fine Arts, Boston, and the Institute of Contemporary Art, a former director of the Boston Society of Architects, and a former chairman of the Boston Foundation for Architecture. On a national level, he is a member of both the National Committee on Design and the distinguished College of Fellows of the American Institute of Architects, and serves as a trustee of the National Building Museum, as well as the National Trust for Historic Preservation. Mr. Gund is a frequent lecturer and speaker and has written and published extensively on architecture and the arts.

Associates

George Coon, ARB
F. Daniel Rutledge, RA
Doris Nelson
David C. Zenk, AIA
Eric Svahn, AIA
Christa M. Mahar
Meng Howe Lim, AIA

John Prokos FAIA
MANAGING PRINCIPAL

In his role as Managing Principal of GUND Partnership, Mr. Prokos effectively leads design exploration, guides the senior design management group and the firm's business practice and is an active member of the firm's Green Design Group. Mr. Prokos is a registered architect in eight states, NCARB certified, a member of the distinguished College of Fellows of the American Institute of Architects, the Boston Society of Architects, and a LEED Accredited Professional.

John has taught at the Boston Architectural College, has been a guest critic at the Harvard Graduate School of Design and Roger Williams University, lectured at Brandeis University and Western Carolina University, and is a frequent invited design juror across the country. His recent invitations include Chair of the AIA Central Tennessee Design Award Jury and Chair of the Washington, D.C. AIA Chapter Design Awards. Currently, Mr. Prokos is the National Architecture Commissioner for the United States Institute of Theater Technology. John serves on the BSA's Nominating Committee and the AIA Governmental Legislative Affairs Committee. John is also a member of the Society for College and University Planning, National Association of Independent Schools and the United States Institute for Theater Technology. He received his Architectural degree from Cornell University, where he also received a postgraduate fellowship to study Mayan architecture of the Yucatan. Prior to joining GUND Partnership in 1984, Mr. Prokos worked with The Architects Collaborative in Cambridge.

Youngmin Jahan AIA
PRINCIPAL

Youngmin Jahan, AIA began working with Graham Gund in 1979 and was named an Associate in 1983, Senior Associate in 1992 and a Principal in 2003. While she primarily focuses on master planning and building designs for colleges and universities, she has built a significant expertise in the design of libraries and science centers. Youngmin is a member of the Society for College and University Planning, the American Institute of Architects, the American Library Association and the Boston Society of Architects.

Ms. Jahan received a Master of Architecture from the Harvard University Graduate School of Design and a Bachelor of Science in Chemistry from Radcliffe College. She is a LEED Accredited Professional. Youngmin has also been involved in the complex repurposing of a number of 1960s buildings on college and university campuses, including the Dimond Library at the University of New Hampshire and the Chemistry Building at Denison University. She has led two national workshops on the topic of 1960s buildings at the national convention of the Society for College and University Planning. She also led a case study of the library and main sciences building at Georgetown University in Washington, D.C. for SCUP in July 2005.

Laura Sanden Cabo AIA
PRINCIPAL

Ms. Cabo joined the firm in 1987, was named an Associate in 1989 and a Principal in 2002. She leads the firm's cultural projects and is an active juror, lecturer and presenter to arts organizations across the United States. Laura is a member of both the American Institute of Architects and the Boston Society of Architects and currently serves on the BSA's Honor Awards Committee.

She received a Bachelor of Arts from Trinity University in San Antonio, Texas and a Master of Architecture from the University of Minnesota under Ralph Rapson. Laura earned accreditation as a LEED Professional in 2004, managing the certification of Washington, D.C.'s first LEED building, the National Association of Realtors headquarters.

Staff
Since 1994

Luann Abrahams
Alahe Aldo
Evelyn Alexandre
Blake Allison
Anthony Anderson
Ingrid Anderson
Gabrielle Angevine
Robert Arthur
Richard Baiano
Jennifer Baker
Sandra Baptie
Derek Barcinski
Katharine Barrows
Julia Shaw-Bartels
John Bates
Marianne Beagan
Russ Beaudin
Cal Beers
Donald Beeson
Lynn Belinsky
Richard Bernstein
Rodrigo Bilbao
Michael Black-Schaffer
Marlon Blackwell
Heather Blair
Michael Blutt
Halee Bouchehrian
Judith Bowen
Constantin Boym
Lance T. Braht
Robert Bramhall
Roland Brito
Lisa Brochu
Donalda Buchanan
Robert Buckham
Jill Buckley
Cathy Busch
Catherine Caddigan
Robert Caddigan
Sara R Caddy
Heather Campbell
Susan Cannon
Donna Carrier
Laura Carthy
Thomas Catalano
Miltos Catomeris
Sheilah Cavanaugh
Daniel Chadwick
Christopher Chan
Frank Chang
Rita Chang
David Choi
Edwin Chung
Yoo Jin Chung
Donna Church
Christopher Clark
Mary Clifford
Katherine Cochran
Lisa Cockerham
Vincent Codispoti
Alexander E. Colt
George P Coon

Marc Cornell
Kimberly A Cowern
Kathyanne Cowles
Nathaniel Cram
William Crozier
James F Cullion
Stephen Dadagian
Eric Daum
Stephanie A. Davis
Pompey Delafield
Kathy Delgreco
Liam Deevy
Michael Dembowski
Paul Demosthenes
Martin Dermady
Sarah Dewey
Katherine Dillon
Kendall Doerr
Susan Doherty
Randy Doi
Mafia Fernandez Donovan
Peter Dubin
Ariel Duren
Miika Ebbrell
Frank Edwards
David Eisen
Amy Eliot
Carl Erikson
Karen Fairbanks
Katherine Faulkner
Vanessa C W Febbo
John Felix
Catherine Fernandez
Joseph Ferraris
Albert Filoni
Dennis Findley
Bells Firkins
Michael Firkins
Donald Flaggs
Matthew Formicola
Christopher Foster
Kierstin Foster
Paul Frazier
Katherine Freygang
Tobias Gabranski
David Gabriel
Donna Gadbois
Joanne Gaines
Evelyn Garber
Christine Garrets
Amy Gendler
Mitt Gess
Donald Gheen
Geraldine Gleason
James Gleason
Ana Gordan
Eric Gould
Ramsay Gourd
Duncan Grant
Sarah Graves
Noah Grunberg
Graham Gund

Mark Haber
Alice Hackman
Barbara Halford
Ellen Harkins
Jane Harrington
Lisa Healy
Robert Heineman
Lizbeth Herbert
Angela Hen-on
Vernon Herzeelle
Arch Hoist
Eric Hollenberg
Debbie Holmes
Lynn Hopkins
Markus Hotz
Tony Hsiao
Carol Hsiung
Frances Chin-Jo Hsu
Lynn Hsu
David Huggins
Christopher Insley
Nicholas Iselin
Susan Israel
Chris Iwerks
Youngmin Jahan
Peter Jelley
Garb Jereczek
Alexandra Johnston
Susan Berger Jones
Math Kaiser
Diane Kasprowicz
Dana Kelly
Edward Kelly
Jiwoon Kim
Joong H Kim
Kenneth Klos
Masatomo Kojima
Joan Koppel
Marsha Kulhonen
Yar Laakso
Margaret Lackner
Manuela LaCount
Jane C Langmuir
Majid Lashkari
Dongik Lee
Samantha Lee
Sang-Yun Lee
Gloria Win LeiLint
Jacob Lilley
Meng Howe Lim
Xiaozhe Lin
Nancy Lippincott
Jay Litman
Hongwei Liu
John Lodge
Kathleen Lugosch
Noah Luken
Rebecca Luther
Elizabeth F Mac Alpine
Jennifer Mack
Sarah MacLaren
Scott MacPherson

Peter E Madsen
Sally Madsen
Christa M Mahar
Tom Maloney
Eric Maltmar
Douglas Manley
Ann Marshall
Carla Turner Mary
Emily Mather
Robert McCauley
Edward McDonald
Paula McGarry
Dee McKee
Jeffrey McLaughlin
Robin Meierding
John Melvin
Honor Merceret
Connie Michener
Holly Miller
Laura Miller
Sara J Miller
Tracy Million
Julie Miner
Jennifer F Mintzer
Ping Mo
Hitomi Mochidome
Kelly Monnahan
Elizabeth Morgan
George Morin
Linda Morrison
Judith Mulhern
Doris Nelson
Lisa Nelson
Sarah Newbury
Thomas Nohr
Charles Nutter
James Nuzum
Bridget E O'Brien
Mart Michael O'Hare
Eric Olsen
Kathleen O'Meara
Ann O'Rahilly
Zobeida Lopez Osorio
Roil Ostberg
John Ostlund
Ivelisse Otero
Megan Ouellette
Richard Panciera
Yunbin Park
Thomas Parks
Alvin Pastrana
Mark Pederson
Dominic Pedulla
Michael Perera
Khalil Pirani
Belly Pisano
Richard Polestio
Donald Potters
John Powell
Donald W Powers
John A Prokos
Kevin Provencher

Timothy Quirk
Denise Randall
Shirley Ransom
Bennett Reed
Ann Marie Reilly
Patrick Reynolds
Mary Anti Rich
Luca Ricco
Sylvia Richards
Jon Richardson
William Ridge
Carlos Ridruejo
Dennis Rieske
Catherine Rintoul
Kenneth Roberts
Pamela Rocheford
Elizabeth Roettger
John Ronan
Michael Rosa
Richard Rosa
Sarah Roszler
Dan Rutledge
Elizabeth Saltonstall
Laura Sanden Cabo
Vincent Santaniello
Christian Santos
Marina Sartori
Kim Schaefer
Graham Schelter
Jennifer Schelter
Kristin Schelter
Benjamin Schreier
Donna Schumacher
Gang Scoby
David Sears
May Ann Sgarlat
Julia Shaw
Howard Shen
William H Sherman
Monica Sidor
Thaddeus Siemasko
Laura Silva
Daniel Simpson
Andrew Skarvinko
Scott Slarsky
Edward J Smith
Jessica Smith
Karen Spence
David Spinelli
James Spinelli
Bony Stanton
Sarah Stanton
Thomas Stark
Madeleine Steczynski
Rachel Steczynski
Bang Stedman
Clark Steven
Margaret Stier
Donna Stillway
Kevin Storm
Jonathan Strand
Margot Street

Raymond A Streeter
Jill Sullivan
Lena Sundgren
Ann Sussman
Eric Svahn
David Tabenken
John Tadewald
Emily Talcott
Susan Tang
Wendy Tardrew
Donald Taylor
Danah Tench
Lynne Thom
Denise Thompson
Hao Tian
Xin Tian
Michael Tingley
Eva Siu Tracy
Pamela Trochesset
Donna L Troiano
James Tsakirgis
Scott Tulay
Luis Valenzuela
Mark Vanderlyn
Sandra Venus
Christine Verbitzki
Carl von Stetten
Philip Wagner
Sharon Walcott
Amy Wales
Mark Wamble
Andrew Wang
Michael Wang
Yali Wang
Xingchen Wang
Catherine Ward
George Warner
Matthew R Wasdyke
Elizabeth Wastler
Paul Weber
Andrew J Weiser
Jackie Welsh
Scott Westerbeke
Kym Wheaton
Charles Willse
Jane Wilson
Justin Winter
Peter Witmer
Vivienne Wong
Xin Yang
Elizabeth Yusem
Jaya Kader Zebede
David Zenk
Gyorgy Zsilak

Current employees are
designated in **bold**

Bibliography

1975–2006

2006

2000 Architects. Aisha, Hasanovi, Ed. Images Publishing Group Vol. 1 (2006): p. 263.

American School & University Magazine. "Architectural Portfolio, Kenyon College, Athletic Center." (August 2006): pp. 134–135.

Thomas, Marita. "Designs Set for $212M Episcopal Academy." *Globest.com* (August 16, 2006).

Beautyman, Mairi. "$212 million Campus Grows Outside Philadelphia." *Interiordesign.com* (August 15, 2006).

Pramik, Mike. "Overhaul on the Oval." *The Columbus Dispatch Business Section Sunday* (July 2, 2006).

Byrum, Marvin. "Forward Progress." *Athletic Business* (June 2006): p. 223.

Edgers, Geoff. "ICA says goodbye to a home that was a little too humble." *The Boston Globe* (June 3, 2006): pp. D1, D6.

Malin, Nadav. "A Beacon for Sustainability." *Green Source, The Magazine of Sustainable Design* (June 2006 Premier Issue): Cover, pp. 57–61.

Miller, Yawu. "Roxbury Lot a Hot Property for Local Development Teams." *The Boston - Baystate Banner* Vol. 41, No. 42 (June 1, 2006).

Reidy, Chris. "3 Teams Bid to Develop Roxbury Site." *Boston Globe* (May 24, 2006).

Fallin, Kevin W. "National Association of Realtors Headquarters, From Brownfield to Green Building to Silver Certification: The Story of Washington, D.C.'s newly constructed LEED-rated Facility." *HPAC Engineering Magazine* (May 2006): Cover, pp. 30–42.

Ingle, Tim. "New Learning Commons Now Open." *The Lantern: The Ohio State Newspaper* (April 7, 2006).

ArchitectureBoston. "2005: The Year in Review." (January/February 2006): pp. 52–53, 87.

New England Real Estate Journal. "Diamond/Sinacori, LLC and E.A. Fish Associates renovating the Waterworks at Chestnut Hill." (January 27, 2006).

2005

American School & University Magazine. "Architectural Portfolio, The Ensworth School." (November 2005): pp. 92–93.

Richardson, John. "Newton." *The Boston Globe* (November 13, 2005).

Radomsky, Rosalie R. "A Shakespeare Garden Heralds Last Act of a Campus Renewal." *The New York Times.*

Prokos, John. "Reminiscences of a Young Architect." *The Architects Collaborative, Reminiscences:* pp. 62–63.

2004

Hillman, Michelle. "Baby Boomers to have their say on luxury condo market." *Boston Business Journal* (October 15, 2004).

Birnbaum, Jeffrey H. "Realtors Wield the Power of Intimidating Views." *Washington Post:* (October 4, 2004): p. E01.

Saunders, Anne. "Waterville Valley shines as smart-growth example." *Seacoastline.com* (August 15, 2004).

Diesenhouse, Susan. "Pumped about the Waterworks." *Boston Globe* (August 14, 2004).

Hedgpeth, Dana. "Hoping Benefits Blooming by Going Green." *Washington Post* (May 17, 2003): p. E03.

Washington Business Journal. "Architecture Winner, Financing Winner." (April 30-May 6, 2004): pp. 6, 10.

ArchitectureBoston. "2003: The Year in Review." (January/February 2004).

Berry College Alumni Magazine. "Founding Fernbank." Vol. 90, No. 2: (Spring 2004): Cover, pp. 12–15.

2003

ArchitectureBoston. "2002: The Year in Review." (January/February 2003): pp. 47, 61.

DuPont's Kitchen and Bath Surfaces. "Architect Graham Gund at home in Nantucket and Cambridge." Issue 1: (2003): pp. 2–9.

Builders Exchange Magazine. "A Jewel-like Glasshouse Offers a Door into Summer." Vol. 2, Issue 4 (April 2003): Cover, pp. 14–21.

Cleveland's Plain Dealer. "The new oasis." (July, 2003). *Architecture.* "On new museums." (August/September 2003): p. 4.

HVAC Engineering. "Systems integration helps glasshouse recreate fragile, biodiverse habitats." (September 2003): pp. 11–12.

Cambridge Tab. "Fall colors turn to art." Vol. 22, No. 3: (September 26, 2003): pp. 1, 3.

Dixon, John Morris. "Campus = Context." *Architecture* (October 2003).

Sullivan, C.C. "Empathy." *Architecture* (October 2003).

Architectural Digest. "Plainly Stated Allowing Architecture to Speak for Itself in Massachusetts." (November 2003): pp. 296–302, 309.

Temin, Christine. "In three exhibits at the Rose, statements in nonconformity." *Boston Sunday Globe* (November 16, 2003): p. N11.

Telegram & Gazette. "Hammers of progress." (December 12, 2003): pp. E1, E10.

2002

Architectural Digest. "AD 100 - Graham Gund." (January 2002): p. 70.

Metropolis. "Big Man On Campus." (January 2002): pp. 54–55.

Hathaway Brown Magazine. "Vision Becomes Reality." Vol. I, Issue I: (2002): pp. 6–11.

Hathaway Brown Magazine. "Designing a Place Where Girls Soar." Vol. I, Issue I: (2002): pp. 12–15.

Dezell, Maureen. "Plans resurface for Paramount facelift." *Boston Globe* (January 12, 2002).

Beacon Hill Times. "A revival for the Paramount Theatre." (January 22, 2002).

Saffron, Inga. "A design that wraps innovation in tradition." *Philadelphia Inquirer* (February 8, 2002).

ArchitecturalRecord.com. "Building Types Study [K - 12]: Hathaway Brown School." (February 2002).

Cambridge Chronicle. "Helping those in need" (April 24, 2002).

Keane, Thomas M. "Hub must act now for theater revival." *Boston Herald* (May 3, 2002).

Taylor, Christie. "By the Seaside, environmentally friendly developments make Panhandle a different kind of Florida." *Boston Herald* (May 23, 2002).

Home Magazine. "Grand Design." (April 2002): pp. 90–95.

Kinzer, Stephen. "An Old Gothic Campus Is Purging Its Architecture of 60's Functionalism." *The New York Times* (July 6, 2002).

The Tennessean. "Ensworth selects designer." (July 16, 2002).

Home Magazine. "Cottage Craft" (July/August 2002): pp. 100–105.

Miller, Yawu. "Developers seek arts center in Lower Rox." *Bay State Banner* (September 19, 2002).

Foster's Daily Democrat. "Berwick Academy dedicates new library" (September 30, 2002).

Architectural Digest. "Graham Gund, An Architect with a Feel for the Past and an Eye on the Future." (November 2002): pp. 146–152.

2001
The Boston Globe. "Fosters' gift to double size of Rose gallery." (January 12, 2001): pp. C1, C7.

Temin, Christine. "At Rose, a pairing of conceptual, contemporary." *Boston Globe* (February 7, 2001).

The Atlanta Constitution. "Fernbank Museum of Natural History." (March 2, 2001): Cover.

Tremblay, Bob. "Rose to blossom with a new wing." *Daily News Sunday* (April 15, 2001).

New England Real Estate Journal. "$14m Smith Hall designed by GUND Partnership: Perini nears completion of 56,000 s/f Holy Cross hall." (June 15, 2001).

Astell, Emilie. "Colleges around city are busy this summer." *Telegram & Gazette* (July 23, 2001).

Horace Mann School Magazine. "Back To The Future: Tillinghast Renovation Will Bring Tomorrow's Technology to This Historic Hall." (Spring 2001): pp. 26–31

Architecture. "William H. Lincoln School Brookline, Massachusetts." (September 2001): pp. 33–35.

Bergeron, Chris. "The Rose is blooming." *Daily News Sunday* (September 30, 2001).

Temin, Christine. "New wing gives Rose room to display its hidden gems." *Boston Globe* (September 28, 2001).

Morgan, William. "Graham Gund's New Art Museum at Brandeis University. Understated grace and classical proportions mark Gund's temple atop the hill." *Art New England* (October/November 2001): p. 6.

Russo, Valerie. "A Rose Grows in Waltham." *Patriot Ledger* (October 6, 2001): pp. 33, 42.

Art New England. "Graham Gund's New Art Museum at Brandeis University." (October/November 2001): p. 6.

Campbell, Robert. "A brave new wing at the Rose Museum." *Boston Sunday Globe* (October 7, 2001).

Desrochers, Donna. "Rose Art Museum draws large crowd for opening of new Lois Foster Wing." *Brandeis Reporter* Vol.19, No. 2 (October 16-November 19, 2001): pp.1, 4.

Holy Cross Magazine. "Smith Hall Dedication." (Fall 2001): pp. 34–39.

Campbell, Robert. "Design Awards make space for beauty and craftsmanship" *Boston Sunday Globe* (December 15, 2001).

New England Real Estate Journal. "Perini Building Co. completes $14 million 56,000 s/f Smith Hall at Holy Cross" (December 21, 2001).

2000
Architectural Digest. "Graham Gund." (January 2000): p. 60.

American School & University Magazine. "University of New Hampshire, Dimond Library, Durham, New Hampshire." (August 2000): p. 50.

ArchitectureBoston. "2000 The Year In Review." (January/February 2000): p. 56.

1999
American School & University Magazine. "University of North Carolina – Chapel Hill, Center Dramatic Art, Chapel Hill, North Carolina." (November 1999): p. 272.

Wood Design & Building. "Nantucket Residence." (Fall 1999): pp. 28–33.

University of New Hampshire Magazine. "Dimond Lights." (November 1999): Cover, pp. 28–31.

1998
Keegan, Edward. "Center for the Performing Arts Skokie, Illinois." *Architecture* (March 1998): pp.110–113.

Faith & Form "What Makes An Exceptional Synagogue?" No. 3, (1998): p. 22.

Bibliography
continued

Contract Design. "Lost and Found." (December 1998): Cover, pp. 16–21.

Builder Magazine. "Island Ensemble" (October 1998): pp. 132–135.

Manforte, Tracy. "Dimond on Display." *UNH Campus Journal* (October 1, 1998): pp. 3–6.

Paine, Maggie. "Graham Gund a Man with a Plan." *UNH Campus Journal* (October 1, 1998): pp. 3, 5.

Perros, Liz. "Public admires Dimond's luster during dedication ceremony." *The New Hampshire* (October 2, 1998): p. 5.

Holl, Jess. "Library Architect Shows Off His Collection (Art and Architecture: A Vision of Graham Gund)." *The New Hampshire* (October 2, 1998): p. B.

1997
Delta Sky Magazine. "Fernbank Museum of Natural History." (February 1997).

O'Donnell, Susannah Cassedy. "Southern Revival: Culture Touring Atlanta." *Cultural Tourism, Museum News, American Association of Museums.* Vol. 76 (January/February 1997): pp. 46–48.

Rodriguez, Alex, "Suburbia's Quiet Cultural Revolution." *Chicago Sun-Times* (April 1997): p. 8.

Critis 97. "Art Buildings And Ideology."

Contract Design. "Law and Disorder." (November 1997).

1996
Architectural Digest. "Graham Gund A Subtle Twist On Convention In Connecticut." (July 1996): pp. 134–139.

Boston Globe Magazine. "Graham Gund" (July 21, 1996).

Kenyon College Alumni Bulletin. "Graham Gund, Architect." Vol. 1, No. 1 (Summer 1996).

Bey, Lee. "Suburbia's Quiet Cultural Revolution." *Chicago Sun-Times* (November 1996): p. 17.

1995
Boston Globe. "A Synagogue Debates a Woman's Place." (May 1995).

Architectural Record. "Endurance Test." (July 1995).

Winchester Star. "Community Benefits to Provide a Home for Autistic Adults." (August 1995).

Architectural Digest. "The AD 100, Graham Gund Architecture." (September 1995).

1994
Southern Accent. "Grand New Opera." (1994).

Historic Preservation. "In The Gund Style." (January/February 1994): pp. 46–53.

Drell, Adrianne. "Skokie Arts Center Plans Unveiled." *Chicago Sun-Times* (October 1994): p. 18.

American School & University Magazine. "Louis I. Kahn Citation." (November 1994).

1993
Boston Arts. "Institute of Contemporary Art." (1993): pp. 376–78.

Wells, J. "On a Human Scale." *The Patriot Ledger-Boston* (1993).

Architectural Record. "Spanning Time." (January 1993): pp. 74–81.

Atlanta Journal/Constitution. "The Scholarship of Science." (January 14, 1993).

Campbell, R. "Fernbank: Life tamed into entertainment." *Boston Globe* (February 19, 1993).

Atlanta Journal/Constitution. "Building Earns Praise." (March 1993).

Architectural Record. "Natural Simulation, Fernbank Museum of Natural History." (May 1993): pp. 80–87.

Decatur Dekalb News. "Fernbank's Kay Davis is a Clever Lady" (May 1993).

Identity Magazine. "All is As It Seams, Blending Architecture and Graphics at an Atlanta Museum." (Summer 1993).

Metropolitan Home. "This Old House." (September/October 1993).

Builder. "Remodeling, Merit Award, The Lansburgh, Washington, D.C." (October 1993): p. 183.

AIA Press. Graham Gund Architects, Foreword by Vincent Scully. (1993).

1992
Theatre Crafts. "DC's Shakespeare Theatre Moves To Lansburgh." (February 1992).

Forgery, B. "Savory Stew – The Lansburgh Building, Mixing It Up." *Washington Post* (February 22, 1992).

Richards, D. "Much Ado About Shakespeare in Washington." *New York Times* (March 15, 1992).

Stone World Magazine. "The Stone Column." (March 1992).

Architecture. "Capital Gains." (April 1992): pp. 74–79.

Architecture. "Bracing History." (April 1992): pp. 85–89.

Building Design & Construction. "The Lansburgh." (October 1992).

Seabrook, C. "At Fernbank, getting it right is all important." *Atlanta Journal/Constitution* (October 3, 1992).

Fox, C. "Museum melds best of old, new." *Atlanta Journal/Constitution* (October 4,1992).

Fox, C. "Design Draws From the Best of Tradition." *Atlanta Journal/Constitution* (October 4,1992).

Gamerman, A. "The High-Tech Approach to the New World Around Us." *Wall Street Journal* (October 27, 1992).

American School & University Magazine. "Mount Holyoke College, Williston Library, South Hadley, Massachusetts." (November 1992): pp. 164–165.

Thieve, J. "By the Yard." *Contract Design* (December 1992): pp. 39–41.

Southern Bell White Pages. (December 1992-93): Cover.

1991
Campbell, R. "Gund's Ballet building is a light delight." *Boston Globe* (July 1991).

Campbell, R. "Concord museum minds its manners too well." *Boston Globe* (October 4, 1991).

Campbell, R. "Harvard Inn has left no room for daring." *Boston Globe* (December 13, 1991).

Chaison, N. "Now for Some Good News: Education Update." *s/f* (March/April 1991).

Clements, J. "Harvard keeping in character with new hotel." *Boston Globe* (August 5, 1991).

Cohen, R. " Two museums: Only one works." *Boston Herald* (April 28, 1991).

Diesenhouse, S. "A High-Tech Ballet Center in Boston." *New York Times* (August 4, 1991).

Fanger, I. " Boston Ballet dances for joy in airy new South End Home." *Sunday Boston Herald* (July 7, 1991).

Gambon, J. "Designing a museum." *Boston Business Journal* (April 29, 1991).

Kay, J.H. "Terms of Endearment." *Architectural Digest* (August 1991): pp. 118–123.

Architectural Digest. "Graham Gund." (August 15, 1991): pp. 106-107.

Taylor, R. "Concord fresh eye on the past." *Boston Globe* (September 21, 1991).

Van Tuyl, L. "A Building Created with Ballet in Mind." *Christian Science Monitor* (July 30, 1991).

Wilson, S. "State Street." *Boston Globe* (January 3, 1991).

Erstein, H. "Scene changes for Shakespeare cast." *Washington Times* (July 30, 1991).

Architecture. "Commercial Washington." (April 1991): p. 57.

1990
Architectural Record. "Town and Country." (February 1990): pp. 128–131.

Campbell, R. "Lincoln Library Wins 'Export Award'." *Boston Globe* (May 8, 1990).

Clipper Magazine. "Graham Gund: The Architect as Developer as Architect." (May 1990): p. 102.

Goldberger, P. "After Opulence, a New 'Lite' Architecture." *New York Times* (May 20, 1990).

Howley, K. "Oasis springs from the ashes." *Boston Herald* (June 29, 1990).

Architecture. "Queen Anne Redux" (July 1990): pp. 74–77.

Architectural Record. "What's This Building Made of?" (July 1990).

Campbell, R. "Architectural promises that go unfulfilled." *Boston Globe* (July 24, 1990).

Building Stone Magazine. "Winning Projects." (July/ August 1990): pp. 30–31.

Architecture. "Team Spirit – Northeastern University Boathouse." (August 1990): pp. 72–75.

Architectural Record. "Theatrical Romance." (August 1990): pp. 83, 90–91.

Westminster Bulletin. "Centennial Center Becomes the Jewel of Our Campus." (Fall, 1990).

Fox, C. "Fernbank Museum Underway." *Atlanta Journal/Constitution* (October 29,1990).

American School & University Magazine. "Northeastern University, Henderson Boathouse." (November 1990): p. 267.

Architecture. "Clothing Store Building." (December 1990): pp. 70– 71.

1989
Tree, C. "Waterville Valley builds a village to remember." *Boston Globe* (February 5, 1989).

Campbell, R. "A cheer for 75 State Street – a winner, warts and all." *Boston Sunday Globe* (April 23, 1989).

A & U. "Boston Architecture – Graham Gund Architects." (April 1989): pp. 87–90.

Goodspeed, L. "One Bowdoin Square: New Look for Historic Location." *s/f* (July/August 1989): pp. 25–26.

Campbell, R. "Gund's Library has a storybook charm." *Boston Globe* (August 1989).

Goldberger, P. "Proof That All That Glitters Is Not Vulgar." *New York Times* (August 13, 1989).

Architectural Record. "Small-town Village." (September 1989): pp. 102–103.

American School & University Magazine. "Architectural Portfolio, Connecticut College Admissions Building." (November 1989): p. 49.

Campbell, R. "Building on a pleasure principle." *Boston Sunday Globe* (December 1989).

Campbell, R. "Glittering & Controversial." *Architecture* (December 1989): pp. 76–79.

Pitoniak, E. "A Touch of New England Class." *Ski* (December 1989): p. 1E–6E.

American School & University Magazine. "Architectural Portfolio, Davidson College Gallery, Art History and Student Arts Facility."

1988
Forgery, B. "Graham Gund's Brave New Buildings." *Washington Post* (January 9, 1988).

Campbell, R. "Architecture: Graham Gund." *Architectural Digest* (February 1988): pp. 128–33.

Progressive Architecture. "Office Building." (February 1988): p. 40.

Baumann, P. "First impressions are important." *The Day* (March 22, 1988).

Von Eackardt, W. "Friend, Lovers and Families." *Washingtonian* (April 1988): p. 76.

Campbell, R. " Graham Gund, A Massachusetts Residence Inspired by Stables." *Architectural Digest* (August 1988): pp. 60–65.

Builder. "Graham Gund – Residence Award." (October 1988): pp.168–69.

Pantridge, M. "Gund's World." *Boston Magazine.* (November 1988).

Radin, C. "A center grows in South Hadley." *Boston Globe* (November 22, 1988).

1987
Campbell, R. "New visitor center upstages Plantation." *Boston Globe* (November 24, 1987).

Cormier, L. "Choreographer of Space: Graham Gund's Museum School Complex." *Art New England* (February 1987): p. 13.

Salisbury, W. "The soaring imagination of a native son." *The Plain Dealer Magazine* (January 11, 1987).

Builder. "Charlestown High School Apartments." (October 1987): pp. 172–73.

American School & University Magazine. "The School of the Museum of Fine Arts Addition and Renovation – Boston, Massachusetts." (November 1987): p. 180.

Progressive Architecture. "Apartment Building- Remodeled Department Store." (August 1987): p. 27.

Home. "Roof with a View." (June 1987): pp. 38–41.

1986
Stange, E. "Brave New Boston." *Boston Herald* (February 16, 1986).

Vogel, C. "A Sense of Place." *New York Times Magazine* Part 2 (April 13, 1986).

Vogel, C. "Summer House by the Sea." *New York Times Magazine* Part 2 (April 13, 1986).

Campbell, R. "Stately Ensemble Unified by a Courtyard," *Architecture* (May 1986): pp. 152–57.

Architectural Record. "Apartment Building – Church Court." (June 1986): p. 97.

Carlock, M. "A new home for the Museum School." *Boston Sunday Globe* (August 3,1986).

Leventhal, E. "How Historic Structures and Modern Needs Can Be Reconciled." *Construction Products Review* (September 1986): pp. 50–53.

Building Stone Magazine. "Whither Post-Modern Architecture?" (Sept/Oct 1996): p. 21.

Builder. "Grand Award – Bulfinch Square." (October 1986): pp. 156–59.

1985
Boles, D. "Assessing a winner." *Progressive Architecture* (February 1985): pp. 88–94.

Campbell, R. "Church Ruins Wall Condominiums." *Architecture* (May 1985): pp. 256–61.

Fisher, T. "Graham Gund Associates – Architects as Developer." *Progressive Architecture* (July 1985): pp. 105–10.

US News & World Report. "Architects Pick the Best of the New." (July 1, 1985).

Mount Holyoke College Art Museum Catalogue. "Architectural Projects by Graham Gund Associates Represented in the Exhibition." (September 1985): pp. 45–51.

Murray, S. "A Change in Vacation Lifestyles." *Homes International* (September/October 1985): pp. 7–13.

Builder. "Townhouses - New Building and Old Church." (October 1985): pp.136–41.

House Beautiful's Building Manual. "Enlivening the Shingle Style." (Fall/Winter 1985-86): pp. 78–81.

Campbell, R. "An original Post–Modernist." *Boston Sunday Globe Magazine* (December 1, 1985).

Temin, C. "The art and architecture of Graham Gund." *Boston Sunday Globe Magazine* (December 1, 1985).

1984
Global Architecture Houses #15. "Summer Residence." (1984): pp. 160–65.

Von Eckardt, W. "Classic Values, New Forms." *Time* (January 2, 1984): pp. 72–73.

Campbell, R. "Church Court – a bright new face on the Boston riverscape." *Boston Globe* (March 4, 1984).

Craig, L. "Alternative Space – Graham Gund." *Art New England* (March 1984): pp. 8–9.

Yudis, A. "A new life for the old Middlesex Courthouse." *Boston Globe* (March 4, 1984).

Vogel, C. "Hanging up a New Shingle." *New York Times Magazine* (April 8, 1984).

Architectural Record. "Private House, Northeastern Coast." (Mid April 1984): pp. 84–87.

Bibliography
continued

Muro, M. "Coverts: Former churches offer unique opportunities for architectural recycling." *Boston Globe* (June 1, 1984).

Baumeister. "Haus in Boston." (July 1984): pp. 40–42.

Baumeister. "Wohnen bei der Kirche in Boston." (July 1984): pp. 61–63.

King, J. "Neighborhood Shaker." *The Patriot Ledger* (October 24, 1984).

1983
House Beautiful's Home Remodeling. "A schoolhouse converted." (Spring 1983): pp. 56–59.

Architectural Record–Record Houses of 1983. "Townhouse renovation, Boston, Massachusetts." (May 1983): pp. 134–37.

The Toshi-Jutaku. "Deutsch House." (November 1983): pp. 43–46.

1982
Housing. "Attic remodeled to a Living Space." (January 1982): p. 101.

Rabinowitz, B. "A New Training Center for the Blind." *The Magazine* (May 1982): pp. 14–18.

Architectural Record. "Classrooms for the blind occupy a renovated stable." (June 1982): pp. 86–89.

Housing. "Remodeled School Building - Cambridge, Massachusetts." (August 1982): p. 51.

1981
Nikkei Architecture. "Schoolhouse condominiums." (1981): pp. 46–47.

Progressive Architecture "Graham Gund Associates: Church Condominiums." (January 1981): pp. 154–55.

Architectural Record. "The Rise and Fall of a 19th Century Schoolhouse – Record Interiors 1981." (February 1981): pp. 70–73.

Campbell, R. "Postmodernism goes to school." *Boston Sunday Globe Magazine* (July 1981).

Baltozer, D. "Graham Gund: quietly shaping the future." *Patriot Ledger* (September 1981).

Lewin, S. "An 1891 Schoolhouse Gears Up for the 20th Century Living." *House Beautiful* (September 1981): pp. 97–99.

1980
Baumeister. "Haus in Massachusetts." (March 1980): pp. 248–251.

Yudis, A. "Perkins school on St. Botolph gets new life." *Boston Sunday Globe* (April 1980).

"Vertical Space: A Service Wing Becomes a Home." *House & Garden* (May-June 1980): pp. 160–163.

L'industria Delle Construzion, Aogosto. "Shapleigh Residence, Massachusetts." (1980): pp. 53–55.

1979
Nikkei Architecture. "Shapleigh Residence." (1979): pp. 5–12.

Architectural Record – Record Houses of 1979. "Shapleigh house on the Massachusetts coast." (May 1979): pp. 50–53.

Guarlnick, E. "A Generational Hideaway." *Boston Sunday Globe Magazine* (August 1979).

The Toshi-Jutako. "Shapleigh House." (October 1979): pp. 5–12.

1978
Progressive Architecture. "De-institutionalizing for the Blind." (April 1978): pp. 92–93.

AIA Journal. "Richardsonian Police Station Becomes a Gallery." (May 1978).

House & Garden. "Back to the Barn." (July 1978): pp. 106–109.

US News and World Report. "When Architects Pick America's Best Buildings." (July 1978).

Morgan, J. "Hyatt Regency Cambridge." *Interiors* (November 1978): pp. 76–79.

Baumeister. "Hotel-Hyatt Regency, Cambridge, Massachusetts." (December 1978): p. 1083.

1977
Architectural Record. "Hyatt Regency Cambridge, A New Shape for an Urban Hotel." (October 1977): pp. 110–113.

1976
Campbell, R. "Stairway for the Starers." *Boston Sunday Globe* (April 1976).

Blake, P. "Constabulary reconsecrated." *Progressive Architecture* (November 1976): p. 45.

Interior Design. "A Permanent Home for the Institute of Contemporary Art." (December 1976): pp. 148–151.

1975
Neely, A. "At Last, the ICA Has Come Home." *The Patriot Ledger* (May 1975).

Rose, B. "Fantasy vs. Reality: The new is conceptual architecture, recycled buildings." *Vogue* (May 1975): p. 28.

Yudis, A. "Recycled Police Station a Haven for Art." *Boston Globe* (April 1975).

Kay, J.H. "New Art Takes Off from Worn-angle Frame." *Boston Globe* (September 1975).

Awards
1975–2007

Kenyon College Athletic Center

Citation, Honor Award for Architecture, Boston Society of Architects
Merit Award for Design Excellence, AIA New England

The Ensworth School, New Campus Development

Honor Award for Architecture, Boston Society of Architects
Honor Award for Design Excellence, American Institute of Architects Tennessee
Citation for Design Excellence, American School and University

National Association of Realtors Headquarters

Presidential Citation for Sustainable Design, Washington DC AIA Chapter
The People's Choice Awards AIA New England Design Awards
Honor Award for Architecture, Boston Society of Architects
American Architecture Awards, The Chicago Athenaeum: Museum of Architecture and Design
Sustainability Awards Citation for Design Excellence, Boston Society of Architects, Committee on the Environment and NYC Chapter American Institute of Architects
Best Architecture Award Best Real Estate Deals, Washington Business Journal
Best Financing Awards Best Real Estate Deals, Washington Business Journal

Friends' Central School Science Center

Historic Preservation Awards Citation for Design Excellence, Lower Merion Historical Architectural Review Board

Westminster School, Athletic Complex

Citation for Design Excellence, American Institute of Architects Connecticut

Denison University, Campus Commons

Honor Award for Design Excellence, American Institute of Architects Ohio

Lois Foster Wing Addition, Rose Art Museum, Brandeis University

Honor Award for Architecture Higher Education Facilities Design Awards, Boston Society of Architects
Honor Award for Architecture, Boston Society of Architects

Carol & Park B. Smith Hall, College of the Holy Cross

Silver Hammer Awards, Worcester Regional Chamber of Commerce
Award for Excellence, Worcester Design Awards

Science & Mathematics Complex, Kenyon College

Higher Education Facilities Design Award for Architecture Design Awards Boston Society of Architects

Hathaway Brown School

Design Excellence for K-12 Schools, Boston Society of Architects

The Waverly at Lake Eola

Aurora Award for Excellence for a "Recreational Facility, Community Clubhouse"
Golden Brick Award, 2002

EuroDisney's International Retail & Manufacturers' Showcase

International Council of Shopping Centers/European Prize

The University of New Hampshire Dimond Library

Excellence in Library Design, American Institute of Architects/American Library Association
Honor Award, Boston Society of Architects / AIA
Award of Merit, Society of American Registered Architects

Lincoln Elementary School

Harleston Parker Award, Boston Society of Architects and the City of Boston
Excellence in Architecture Award, New England Regional Council / AIA
AIA Honor Award, Boston Society of Architects
Citation, American School and University

St. Paul's School, Kehaya House Dormitory

Award of Excellence, Society of American Registered Architects
Housing Award, Boston Society of Architects / AIA

Firm Award

Award of Excellence, Society of American Registered Architects

The Nantucket Residence

AIA Housing Award, Boston Society of Architects

Westminster School Edge House Dormitory

AIA Housing Award, Boston Society of Architects

The Shubert Theatre

Merit Award, United States Institute for Theatre Technology

Connecticut College Horizon Admissions Building

Citation, American School and University

Connecticut College Blaustein Humanities Center

Citation, American School and University
Exports Award, Boston Society of Architects

Davidson College Visual Arts Center

Louis Kahn Citation, American School and University

Northeastern University Henderson Boathouse

Excellence in Architecture Award, New England
 Regional Council / AIA
Citation, American School and University

School of the Museum of Fine Arts

Award for Conservation, Victorian Society, New
 England Chapter First Award/Design, International
 Masonry Institute

**The Westminster School Centennial Performing Arts
Center**

Award of Excellence, National Commercial Builders
 Council

Bostix Pavilion

International Illumination Design Award
Honor Award, Boston Society of Architects / AIA
Excellence in Architecture Award, New England
 Regional Council / AIA

Boston Ballet Studios & Offices

Award of Excellence, National Commercial Builders
 Council

Bulfinch Square

Excellence in Architecture Award, New England
 Regional Council / AIA
Award for Conservation, Victorian Society, New
 England Chapter
Grand Award, Builder's Choice

Carroll Center for the Blind

Excellence in Architecture Award, New England
 Regional Council / AIA

Church Court

Honor Award for Excellence in Design, American Insti-
 tute of Architects
Housing Award, Boston Society of Architects
Project of the Year, Builder's Choice
Harleston Parker Medal, Boston Society of Architects
Excellence in Architecture Award, New England
 Regional Council / AIA
Best Designs of the Year, Time Magazine
Progressive Architecture Design Citation

Disney's Florida Beach Resort

Award of Merit, Palm Beach Regional Council / AIA

Enders Residence

Grand Award, Builder's Choice Design & Planning
 Awards

Fernbank Museum of Natural History

Excellence in Architecture Award, New England
 Regional Council / AIA

Hyatt Regency Cambridge

Environmental Improvement Award, Landscape Contrac-
 tors of America
Interior Design Award, Institutions Magazine
Outstanding Design Award, Massachusetts Masonry
 Institute
Honor Award for Excellence in Design, American Insti-
 tute of Architects

The Lansburgh

Merit Award, Builder's Choice

Lincoln Library

Excellence in Architecture Award, New England
 Regional Council / AIA
Exports Award, Boston Society of Architects

Nesbeda Residence

Merit Award, Builder's Choice

One Faneuil Hall Square

Project Excellence Award, National Association of
 Industrial and Office Parks

Seventy-Five State Street

Craft Award, Best Marble Project, International Union
 Bricklayers & Allied Craftsmen
International Masonry Institute First Place Award
Tucker Architectural Award, Building Stone Institute

The School-House

Housing First Honor Award, American Institute of
 Architects
Record Interiors, Architectural Record
Housing Award, Boston Society of Architects
Excellence in Architecture Award, New England
 Regional Council / AIA
Design Excellence in Housing Award, Boston Society of
 Architects

Shapleigh Summer Residence

Housing Award of Merit, American Institute of Archi-
 tects
Housing Award, Boston Society of Architects
Excellence in Architecture Award, New England
 Regional Council / AIA
Record Houses, Architectural Record

Deutsch Residence

Record Houses, Architectural Record
Excellence in Architecture Award, New England
 Regional Council / AIA

Project Chronology
1973–2008

1973
Private Residence, Aspen, Colorado
Rockefeller Residence, Cambridge, Massachusetts

1974
Coppermine Farm Barn, Guest House, Griggstown, New Jersey

1975
Massachusetts Association for Blind, Life Learning Center, Project, Boston, Massachusetts

1976
Hyatt Regency Cambridge Hotel, Cambridge, Massachusetts
Institute of Contemporary Art, Boston, Massachusetts

1977
Waterfront Hotel, Project, Boston, Massachusetts

1978
Shapleigh Summer Residence, Mishaum Point, Massachusetts
Webster Spring Company, Project, Washington, D.C.
Willard Place/Dunfey Hotels, Project, Washington, D.C.

1979
The School-House Condominiums, Boston, Massachusetts
Old Port Hotel, Project, Portland, Maine

1980
Harvard University Squash Courts, Feasibility Study, Cambridge, Massachusetts
Sargent's Wharf, Project, Boston, Massachusetts
Wentworth-By-The-Sea, Project, Portsmouth, New Hampshire

1981
Boston Society of Architects, The Architectural Bookstore, Boston, Massachusetts
City of Boston School Reuse Survey, Boston, Massachusetts
Bowditch Park, Project, Salem, Massachusetts

1982
Synectics, Offices, Cambridge, Massachusetts
Engelhard Residence, Project, Cambridge, Massachusetts
Creek Square, Project, Boston, Massachusetts

1983
Church Court, Boston, Massachusetts
Deutsh Residence, South Dartmouth, Massachusetts
Davis Residence, South Dartmouth, Massachusetts
Patterson Residence, Fisher's Island, New York
Harvard University, Johnston Gatehouse, Cambridge, Massachusetts
Allegheny County Jail & Courthouse, Feasibility Study, Pittsburgh, Pennsylvania

1984
Bulfinch Square, Cambridge, Massachusetts
Carroll Center for the Blind, Newton, Massachusetts
Hyatt Regency Cambridge Hotel, Health Club, Cambridge, Massachusetts
South End, Master Plan, Boston, Massachusetts
Stone Zoo, Master Plan, Stoneham, Massachusetts
Zero Arrow Street, Project, Cambridge, Massachusetts
Earthwatch, Project, Boston, Massachusetts
95 Berkeley Street, Project, Cambridge, Massachusetts
Frontage Road Office Building, Project, Boston, Massachusetts

1985
Arnot Art Museum, Elmira, New York
678 Massachusetts Avenue, Cambridge, Massachusetts
Riverwalk Hotel, Project, Lawrence, Massachusetts
First National Bank of Ipswich, Project, Ipswich, Massachusetts

Shapleigh Summer Residence

The Hyatt Hotel at Cambridge

Cohen Residence

75 State Street

The Inn at Harvard

Fernbank Museum of Natural History

1986
Connecticut College, Blaustein Center for the Humanities, New London, Connecticut
Cohen Residence, Boston, Massachusetts
Nesbeda Residence, Harvard, Massachusetts
Fuller Block, Boston, Massachusetts
Radcliffe College, Bunting Institute, Cambridge, Massachusetts
90 Canal Street, Boston, Massachusetts
Osterville Town Center, Feasibility Study, Osterville, Massachusetts
Boston Center for Arts, Master Plan, Boston, Massachusetts
161 First Street, Cambridge, Massachusetts
Cone Condominiums Offices, Boston, Massachusetts
Newharbor, Master Plan, Providence, Rhode Island
25 Huntington Avenue, Project, Boston, Massachusetts
Lowell Mills Project, Lowell, Massachusetts

1987
9-11 Mt. Auburn Street, Cambridge, Massachusetts
Plimoth Plantation Visitors Center, Plymouth, Massachusetts
School of the Museum of Fine Arts, Boston, Massachusetts
The School-House on Monument Square, Charlestown, Massachusetts
Battery Wharf, Project, Boston, Massachusetts

1988
Maritime Center at Norwalk, Norwalk, Connecticut
One Faneuil Hall Square, Boston, Massachusetts
600 Memorial Drive, Boston, Massachusetts
Congress Street Pedestrian Overpass, Feasibility Study, Boston, Massachusetts
Merchants Row, Boston, Massachusetts
Clarendon Square, Project, Boston, Massachusetts

1989
Waterville Valley Town Square, Waterville Valley, New Hampshire
Golden Eagle Lodge, Waterville Valley, New Hampshire
Seventy-Five State Street, Boston, Massachusetts with
 Skidmore, Owings and Merrill, Architect & Engineers
Lincoln Library, Lincoln, Massachusetts
Westminster School, Centennial Performing Arts Center, Simsbury, Connecticut
Connecticut College, Horizon Admissions Building, New London, Connecticut
Shapleigh Residence, Ladue, Missouri
Northeastern University, Henderson Boathouse, Boston, Massachusetts
One Bowdoin Square, Boston, Massachusetts
Cardinal Cushing Park, Boston, Massachusetts
Spiro Residence, Edgartown, Massachusetts
Massachusetts General Hospital, Alzheimer's Disease Care Center,
 Feasibility Study, Boston, Massachusetts
Dalton Street Housing, Project, Boston, Massachusetts
Lewis Wharf, Project, Boston, Massachusetts

1990
University of New Hampshire, Library Feasibility Study, Durham, New Hampshire
American University, Performing Arts Center, Project, Washington, D.C.
Society for the Preservation of New England Antiquities, Conservation Center, Project,
 Waltham, Massachusetts
Massachusetts General Hospital, Master Plan & Feasibility Study, Boston, Massachusetts
The Channing House, Project, Cambridge, Massachusetts
Museum of American Textile History, Project, Lawrence, Massachusetts

1991
Concord Museum, Concord, Massachusetts
The Village Commons, South Hadley, Massachusetts
The Lansburgh, Washington, D.C.
Boston Ballet, Boston, Massachusetts
Mt. Holyoke College, Williston Library, South Hadley, Massachusetts
The Inn at Harvard, Cambridge, Massachusetts
Rockefeller Residence Addition, Cambridge, Massachusetts
Inn at Kennebunkport, Feasibility Study, Kennebunkport, Maine

North Shore Performing Arts Center

Cheekwood Museum + Visitor Center

Taft School Library

Westminster School Squash Pavilion

1992
Fernbank Museum of Natural History, Atlanta, Georgia
University of The South, Gailor Hall, Project, Sewanee, Tennessee
University of The South, Studio Arts Building Project, Sewanee, Tennessee
Concord Academy, Dormitory, Project, Concord, Massachusetts
The Ski Market, Feasibility Study, Brookline, Massachusetts
Westminster School, Cushing Hall, Master Plan, Simsbury, Connecticut
This Old House, Lexington, Massachusetts

1993
Davidson College, Visual Arts Center, Davidson, North Carolina
Enders Residence, Waterford, Connecticut
Museum of Cape Ann History, Gloucester, Massachusetts
The William H. Lincoln School, Brookline, Massachusetts
Harrison Opera House Norfolk, Virginia with Williams, Tazewell and Associates, Architect
St. Paul's School, Kehaya House, Concord, New Hampshire
Disney Vacation Club, Indian River County, Florida
Woods Hole Oceanographic Institute, Discovery Center, Feasibility Study, Woods Hole, Massachusetts

1994
Centre East Performing Arts Center, Skokie, Illinois
Disney Resort and Convention Center, Lake Buena Vista, Florida
The Nantucket House, Nantucket, Massachusetts
The Lawrenceville School, Library, Lawrenceville, New Jersey
Boch Center for the Performing Arts, Master Plan, Mashpee, Massachusetts
Rehabilitation Hospital of the Cape and Islands, Sandwich, Massachusetts
Case Western Reserve University, Law School, Cleveland, Ohio
The Lawrenceville School, Music Building, Lawrenceville, New Jersey
Franklin Park Zoo, Predator/Prey Exhibit, Boston, Massachusetts
Cheekwood Museum and Botanical Gardens, Nashville, Tennessee
St. Paul's School, Armour Dormitory, Concord, New Hampshire
80 Broad Street, Boston, Massachusetts

1995
Disney's Florida Beach Resort, Vero Beach, Florida

1996
Young Israel Synagogue, Brookline, Massachusetts
North Shore Center for the Performing Arts, Skokie, Illinois
Shubert Theater Renovation, Boston, Massachusetts
Summer Residence, Nantucket, Massachusetts
Westminster School, Memorial Hall Dormitory Renovation, Simsbury, Connecticut

1997
All Saints' Episcopal Church, South Hadley, Massachusetts
Disney's Coronado Springs Resort and Convention Center, Orlando, Florida
Florence Sawyer Elementary School, Bolton, Massachusetts
The Taft School, Master Plan, Watertown, Connecticut
The Taft School, Library, Mathematics and Science Building, Watertown, Connecticut
Law School Library Addition, Case Western Reserve University, Cleveland, Ohio
Culver Academy, Legion Memorial Building Renovation, Culver, Indiana
The Park School Expansion, Brookline, Massachusetts
Portsmouth Public Library, Portsmouth, New Hampshire

1998
Lawrenceville School, Visual Arts Building and Library, Lawrenceville, New Jersey
University of New Hampshire, Dimond Library, Durham, New Hampshire
Concord Academy, Student Health and Athletic Complex, Concord, Massachusetts
Northeastern University, Henderson Boathouse, Boston, Massachusetts

1999

Brandeis University, Master Plan, Waltham, Massachusetts
University of North Carolina, Center for Dramatic Arts, Chapel Hill, North Carolina
Disney Inn, Celebration, Florida
Berwick Academy, Jeppesen Science Center, South Berwick, Maine
Longyear Residence Study, Brookline, Massachusetts
Newburyport Inn Study, Newburyport, Massachusetts
Saint Paul Academy and Summit School Expansion, St. Paul, Minnesota
Stratton Mountain Village Common, Stratton, Vermont
The Taft School, Art Gallery Study, Watertown, Connecticut
The Village at Spruce Peak Master Plan Study, Stowe Mountain, Vermont
The Winsor School Theater Master Plan, Boston, Massachusetts
Charles Street Jail Re-use Master Plan, Boston, Massachusetts

Horace Mann School

2000

Kenyon College, Eaton Center, Gambier, Ohio
Inn at Celebration, Celebration, Florida
Kenyon College, Music Building, Gambier, Ohio
Westminster School, Squash Pavilion, Simsbury, Connecticut
St. John's School, Virginia Tatham Fine Arts Center, Houston, Texas
The Taft School, Dining Hall Study, Watertown, Connecticut
New Jewish High School Master Plan, Waltham, Massachusetts
North Shore Music Theater Master Plan, Beverly, Massachusetts
Westover School Master Plan, Middlebury, Connecticut

The Ensworth School

2001

Hathaway Brown School, Middle School Complex, Shaker Heights, Ohio
Kenyon College, Mathematics and Science Complex, Gambier, Ohio
College of the Holy Cross, Carol and Park B. Smith Hall, Worcester, Massachusetts
Five Lowell Street Residence, Cambridge, Massachusetts
Friends' Central School Master Plan, Wynnewood, Pennsylvania
EuroDisney's International Retail and Manufacturers' Showcase, Paris, France
The Waverly at Lake Eola, Orlando, Florida
Kehillath Israel Synagogue Master Plan, Brookline, Massachusetts
LA Excels Master Plan, Lewiston, Maine
Lois Foster Wing at the Rose Art Museum, Waltham, Massachusetts
National Center for Afro-American Artists, Parcel 3, Boston, Massachusetts
The Taft School, Ice Hockey Rink, Watertown, Connecticut
Westover School, Athletic Complex, Middlebury, Connecticut
Virginia Military Institute, Fine Arts Center Master Plan, Lexington, Virginia
WaterColor Town Center Condominiums, St Joe Towns and Resorts, Water Color, Florida
Wells College Master Plan, Aurora, New York

Denison University Campus Common

2002

Accelerace Study, Paris, France
Horace Mann School, Riverdale, New York
Berwick Academy, Jackson Library, South Berwick, Maine
Celebration Office Building, Celebration, Florida
Celebration High School, Celebration, Florida
Cornell University Community Recreation Center Master Plan Study, Ithaca, New York
Spartanburg Cultural Arts Center Study, Spartanburg, South Carolina
Sweet Briar College, Student Commons, Sweet Briar, Virginia

2003

Bayside Village Center Master Plan, Virginia Beach, Virginia
Episcopal Academy Master Plan, Merion, Pennsylvania
The Fannie Cox Center for Science, Math and Technology, Friends' Central School, Wynnewood, Pennsylvania
WaterSound Bridges, WaterSound, Florida
Denison University, Burton D. Morgan Hall, Granville, Ohio
Denison University, Talbot Hall of Biological Sciences, Granville, Ohio
Denison University, Chemistry Building, Granville, Ohio (design)
Cleveland Botanical Garden, Cleveland, Ohio
Westminster School, Pool Pavilion, Simsbury, Connecticut
The Crossings, St. Joe Towns and Resorts, WaterSound, Florida

Friends' Central School

2004

Bronx Zoo Butterfly House, Bronx, New York
Compass Point II, St Joe Towns and Resorts, WaterSound, Florida
Disney's Saratoga Spring Resort & Spa, Orlando, Florida
The Ensworth School, Nashville, Tennessee
National Association of Realtors, Washington, D.C.
Tufts University, Solar Dormitory Study, Medford, Massachusetts
Kenyon College, Housing Master Plan, Gambier, Ohio
Western Carolina University, Fine and Performing Arts Center, Cullowhee, North Carolina

Western Carolina University

2005

Bostix Pavilion Expansion Study, Boston, Massachusetts
Kenyon College, Kenyon Athletic Center, Gambier, Ohio
The Groton School, Campbell Center for the Performing Arts, Groton, Massachusetts
Hathaway Brown School, Carol and John Butler Aquatic Center, Shaker Heights, Ohio
Episcopal High School, Baker Science Center, Alexandria, Virginia
Carleton College, Arts Master Plan, Northfield, Minnesota
KI Synagogue, Elevator Addition, Brookline, Massachusetts
Polly Hill Arboretum, Planning Study, Edgartown, Massachusetts

2006

Disney's Core Services, Grand Central Creative Campus Office Buildings, Glendale, California
The Webb School, Science Building, Knoxville, Tennessee
New Orleans Housing and Redevelopment Competition, New Orleans, Louisiana
Crescent Keel Cottages, St. Joe Towns and Resorts, WaterSound, Florida
The Gatehouse, St. Joe Towns and Resorts, WaterSound, Florida
WaterSound West Beach Pool House and Mail Kiosk, St. Joe Towns and Resorts, WaterSound, Florida

University of Massachusetts Visual Arts Center

2007

Copley Square MBTA Station, Boston, Massachusetts
The Waterworks at Chestnut Hill Housing Development, Chestnut Hill, Massachusetts
Young Israel New Rochelle Synagogue, New Rochelle, New York
Kenyon College, Peirce Dining Hall, Gambier, Ohio
Iron Mountain House, Kent, Connecticut
Private Residence, Stowe, Vermont

2008–beyond

South Franklin Circle Senior Community Development, Chagrin Falls, Ohio
Disney's Vacation Club & Resort at Eagle Pines, Orlando, Florida
Emory University, Oxford College Library and IT Center, Atlanta, Georgia
The Ensworth School, Theater, Nashville, Tennessee
Harrison Avenue Housing Development, Boston, Massachusetts
The Ohio State University, Thompson Library Addition and Renovation, Columbus, Ohio
University of Massachusetts, Visual Arts Center, Amherst, Massachusetts
San Marco Mixed Use Housing Development, Jacksonville, Florida
Episcopal Academy, Student Center, Merion, Pennsylvania
Kenyon College, Visual Arts Center, Gambier, Ohio
Newton North High School, Newton, Massachusetts
Westminster School, Academic Building, Simsbury, Connecticut
The Rashi School, Dedham, Massachusetts
Rippowam Cisqua High School, Bedford, New York
Martha's Vineyard Historical Society Museum, Edgartown, Massachusetts
Private Residence, Gambier, Ohio
Macalester College, Fine and Performing Arts Center, St. Paul, Minnesota
The Taft School, Dining Hall Expansion, Watertown, Connecticut
National Center for Afro-American Artists, Roxbury, Massachusetts

The Ohio State University, Thompson Library

Acknowledgements

Every architectural practice is a collaborative endeavor, filled with the ebb and flow of many skilled participants. We are especially grateful for the tapestry of clients, consultants and collaborators who have labored to make the building process one of discovery, joy and purpose.

Our ability to explore, grow and evolve is due in no small measure to the stability and strength of our principal and associate group, who bring an average tenure of more than fifteen years working together in our practice. This talented, stalwart group continues to bring new ideas, as well as an uncommon respect and dignity, to a sometimes complex process. I owe them all a great debt of gratitude for their selfless commitment to this shared vision.

Carlos Ridruejo brought an elegant and sure hand to the design of this monograph. Christa Mahar managed the enormous task of marrying words with images.

To each person who has traveled part of this fascinating course with me, I do hope you have enjoyed the journey as much as I.

Graham Gund, FAIA
Cambridge, Massachusetts
December 2007

Photography Credits

Cleveland Botanical Garden
Jeff Goldberg/Esto, Cover and Title Pages

Brandeis University, Lois Foster Wing, Rose Art Museum
Bruce Martin, p. 7

Kenyon College Athletic Center
David Lamb, p. 11

Hathaway Brown School Middle School
Jonathan Hillyer, pp. 17, 18 (1), 19 (1), 20 (1, 2), 22 (1)
Chuck Choi, pp. 21, 22–23 (1)
courtesy The Albert M. Higley Co., p. 18 (2)

Hathaway Brown School Pool Pavilion
Chuck Choi, pp. 25–29

Horace Mann School
Jeff Goldberg/Esto, pp. 31–37

The Ensworth School
Jeff Goldberg/Esto, pp. 39, 41–47
Peter Vanderwarker, p. 40 (1)

The Taft School Library, Mathematics and Science Building
Peter Aaron/Esto, pp. 49–53

Friends' Central School Fannie Cox Center
Chuck Choi, pp. 55–57

Lawrenceville School Visual Arts Center and Library
Warren Jagger, pp. 59–61
Nick Wheeler, pp. 62–63

Young Israel Synagogue
Steve Rosenthal, pp. 65–69

University of North Carolina Chapel Hill, Center for Dramatic Arts
Jonathan Hillyer, pp. 71–77

Inn at Celebration
Robert Benson, pp. 79–81

WaterSound Bridges
courtesy Contech, p. 81
Smith Aerial Photography, pp. 84–85

Kenyon College Eaton Center
Jonathan Hillyer, pp. 85–89

University of New Hampshire, Dimond Library
Nick Wheeler, pp. 91, 93 (1), 94 (2), 95
Bruce Martin, p. 92 (1,2)
Michael Warren, p. 94 (1)

Kenyon College Science and Mathematics Buildings
Jonathan Hillyer, pp. 97–103

Berwick Academy Science Center
Anton Grassl, pp. 105–107

Berwick Academy Library
Brian Vanden Brink, pp. 109, 110 (1)
Andrew Barresi, pp. 110–111

Kenyon College Music Building
David Lamb, p. 113
Jonathan Hillyer, pp. 114–117

North Shore Center for the Performing Arts
Hedrich-Blessing, pp. 119-121

Groton School Campbell Performing Arts Center
Peter Vanderwarker, pp. 123–125

College of the Holy Cross, Smith Hall
Jeff Goldberg/Esto, pp. 135, 136 (1), 137–141
courtesy College of the Holy Cross, p. 136 (2)

Denison University, Burton D. Morgan Building and Talbot Hall
Jeff Goldberg/Esto, pp. 129–147
courtesy Denison University, p. 130 (2)

Episcopal High School, Baker Science Center
Michael Dersin, pp. 149–150 (1), 151
courtesy Episcopal High School, p. 150 (2)

Private Residence, Nantucket, Massachusetts
Peter Aaron/Esto, pp. 153–157

Private Residence, Cambridge, Massachusetts
Peter Aaron/Esto, pp. 158–165

Celebration Office Buildings
Robert Benson, pp. 167–171

Celebration High School
Robert Benson, pp. 173–179

Cleveland Botanical Garden
Jeff Goldberg/Esto, pp. 181–182, 183 (3), 184–185, 186 (1), 187–191
Eric Svahn, p. 183 (1)
rendering by Xingchen Wang, p. 186 (2)

Case Western Reserve University Law Library
Nick Wheeler, pp. 193–195

EuroDisney
courtesy LaVallee, pp. 197–201

The Waverly at Lake Eola
courtesy ZOM Development, pp. 203–205

National Association of Realtors Building
Alan Karchmer, pp. 207, 209, 210 (4), 211, 212–214
Robert C. Lautman, pp. 208 (1,2), 210 (1)
courtesy NAR, p. 208 (3)

Ohio State University Thompson Library
renderings by Xin Tian, pp. 217–221
courtesy Ohio State University, p. 218 (1)

Brandeis University, Lois Foster Wing, Rose Art Museum
Jonathan Hillyer, pp. 223–225, 228 (3), 229
Bruce Martin, pp. 226–227
Carlos Ridruejo, p. 228 (2,4)
courtesy Boston Globe, p. 229

Kenyon College Athletic Center
David Lamb, pp. 231–247

Copley T Station
renderings by Matt Formicola, pp. 250–251

Tufts University Housing Study
renderings by Jon Richardson, pp. 252–253

Denison University Chemistry Building
renderings by Xin Tian, pp. 254–255

University of Massachusetts, Amherst Visual Arts Building
renderings by Matt Formicola, pp. 256–257

Newton North High School
renderings by Xin Tian, pp. 258–259

GUND Partnership Offices
Christa Mahar, p. 263
Chuck Choi, p. 265, 266 (1,2)

GUND Partnership Portraits
Mark Ostow, pp. 267–269, 271

Project Chronology
Shapleigh Summer Residence, Steve Rosenthal, p. 280
Hyatt Regency, Steve Rosenthal, p. 280
Cohen Residence, Warren Jagger Photography, p. 281
75 State Street, Steve Rosenthal, p. 281
The Inn at Harvard, Warren Jagger Photography, p. 281
Fernbank Museum of Natural History, Jonathan Hillyer, p. 281
North Shore Performing Arts Center, Jon Miller, Hedrich-Blessing, p. 282
Cheekwood Museum, Jonathan Hillyer, p. 282
The Taft School Library, Peter Aaron/Esto, p. 282
Westminster School Squash Pavilion, Steve Rosenthal, p. 282
Horace Mann School, Jeff Goldberg/Esto, p. 283
The Ensworth School, Jeff Goldberg/Esto, p. 283
Denison University Campus Common, Jeff Goldberg/Esto, p. 283
The Friends' School, Chuck Choi, p. 283
Western Carolina University, courtesy WCU, p. 284
University of Massachusetts, rendering by Matthew Formicola, p. 284
Ohio State University, rendering by Xin Tian, p. 284
Kenyon College Athletic Center, David Lamb, p. 285

Endpapers
Kenyon College Athletic Center, David Lamb

We would like to acknowledge the fine work of these professionals and their permission to reproduce the images in this collection. All efforts have been made to trace original source material.

Acknowledgements 286

Athletics Centers 24, 230

Awards 278

Baker Science Center, Episcopal High School 148

Berwick Academy 104, 108

Bibliography 272

Botanical Gardens 180

Brandeis University 222

Burton D. Morgan Hall, Denison University 134

Campbell Center for the Performing Arts, The Groton School 122

Carol and John Butler Aquatic Center, Hathaway Brown School 24

Carol and Park B. Smith Hall, College of the Holy Cross 126

Case Western Reserve University 192

Celebration High School 172

Celebration Office Building 166

Center for Dramatic Arts, University of North Carolina 70

Chemistry Building, Denison University 254

Cleveland Botanical Garden 180

Collaboration by Design 262

College and University 70, 86, 90, 96, 112, 122, 126, 134, 142, 192, 216, 222, 230, 252, 254, 256

College of the Holy Cross 126

Commercial and Office Buildings 78, 166, 196, 206

Copley Square Subway Station 250

Denison University 134, 142, 254

Dimond Library, University of New Hampshire 90

Eaton Center, Kenyon College 86

Episcopal High School 148

EuroDisney's International Retail and Manufacturers' Showcase 196

Fine and Performing Arts 58, 70, 112, 118, 122, 222, 256, 260

Five Lowell Street Residence 158

Friends' Central School 54

Firm Profile 264

Goldberger, Paul 6

Gund, Graham 6, 264, 268, 288

Hathaway Brown School 16, 24

High Schools 148, 172, 258

Horace Mann School 30

Housing 82, 86, 202, 252

Housing Study, Tufts University 252

Independent Schools 16, 24, 30, 38, 48, 54, 58, 104, 108

Inn at Celebration 78

Jackson Library, Berwick Academy 108

Jeppesen Science Center, Berwick Academy 104

Kenyon Athletic Center, Kenyon College 230

Kenyon College 86, 96, 112, 230

Law School Library Addition, Case Western Reserve University 192

Lawrenceville School 58

Lewis, Hilary 264

Libraries 48, 58, 90, 108, 192, 216

Library, Mathematics and Science Building, The Taft School 48

Lois Foster Wing at the Rose Art Museum 222

Mathematics and Science Complex, Kenyon College 96

Middle School Complex, Hathaway Brown School 16

Museums 222

Music Building, Kenyon College 112

National Association of Realtors 206

National Center for Afro-American Artists 260

Newton North High School 258

North Shore Center for the Performing Arts 118

Photography Credits 287

Project Chronology 280

Residences 152, 158

Schools (all) 16, 24, 30, 38, 48, 54, 58, 104, 108, 148, 172, 258

Science Buildings/Laboratories 48, 54, 96, 104, 142, 148, 254

Subway Stations 250

Summer Residence, Nantucket, Massachusetts 152

Talbot Hall of Biological Science, Denison University 142

The Ensworth School 38

The Fannie Cox Center for Math and Technology, Friends' Central School 54

The Groton School 122

The Ohio State University 216

The Taft School 48

The Waverly at Lake Eola 202

Thompson Library Addition and Renovation, The Ohio State University 216

Tufts University 252

Universities and Colleges 70, 86, 90, 96, 112, 122, 126, 134, 142, 192, 216, 222, 230, 252, 254, 256

University of Massachusetts 256

University of New Hampshire 90

University of North Carolina 70

Visual Arts Building and Library, Lawrenceville School 58

Visual Arts Center, University of Massachusetts 256

WaterSound Bridges 82

Young Israel Synagogue 64

Index